A Bathtub in Our Kitchen

Robert W. Martin

First paperback edition printed 2016 in the United Kingdom
Second edition 2025
ISBN 978-0-9928974-4-4
© Robert W. Martin.

Published by Linear Road Press
Suite 10544
PO Box 6945
London W1A 6US

For more copies of this book, please email
info@la-darnoire.com
Although every precaution has been taken in the preparation of this book, the publisher and author assume no responsibility for errors or omissions. Neither is any liability assumed for damages resulting from the use of any information contained herein.

In memory of my mother,
who instilled in me a love for the written word.

Preface

P RIOR to writing the first book, I had no idea that a bathtub would become such a central feature. As there was very little literature in English regarding the region of Sologne, I initially intended to simply introduce readers to this area; something along the lines of "A Year in Sologne". However, as the first year progressed, my perspective changed. Because the ancient farmhouse into which we had moved lacked even the most basic of amenities, the focus switched from the region itself to a more personal goal; achieving the luxury of an indoor bathroom.

However, due to other priorities (including being as self-sufficient as possible, as cheaply as possible) the construction of a bathroom took a lot longer than we thought.

Because we sold our house in the UK during a buyers' market, we did not have pots of money to lavishly spend on upgrading our home. To save money, every improvement to the house has been done by my wife and I; although the occasional assistance from a distant neighbour was sometimes necessary!

As well as the upgrading of the building itself, the aged Father-in-law (FIL for short) was another problem with which we had to cope. He is bedridden; this was one of the reasons for us moving to France. Fortunately the property has two houses – we would not have moved to France at all if we had had to live with him in the same house! To say he is a difficult character would be an understatement. As to why he's bedridden – it started off by being a psychological problem. He's not that old – only 78. You see, he's not very steady on his legs, due to an accident with a piece of earthmoving equipment. Before we came to France, he contracted a stomach bug. Because food was making him ill, he decided to stop eating. Of course this meant he became quite weak, and when he fell over in the kitchen, he found he couldn't get up again. He spent the winter's night on the cold tiles of the kitchen floor, and was found the following morning by M&O (the chief hunter and his wife). After several weeks in hospital, he returned home – this was shortly after we moved here. Since then, his fear of falling over meant he decided to stay in bed. Of course, the more he stays in bed, the weaker he becomes. So the problem is now physical as well.

Our first experience with the legendary French bureaucracy came when we re-registered our vehicles in France. Since then, we know what to expect as far as paperwork is concerned. Although I can now read French, and carry out a conversation – albeit with horribly mangled grammar – my form-filling skills are far from satisfactory. So this added burden falls on my wife, LSS (Long-Suffering Spouse).

By the end of the first year, several stages of the renovation project had been completed. The house had gutters, which diverted rainwater into large holding tanks. We had a borehole and clean water on tap in the kitchen. A thermal store had been constructed ready to provide hot water for the household via a boiler stove. The electrical wiring had been upgraded and was now compliant with modern standards – and oh, the joy of having proper electrical sockets everywhere instead of dozens of plugs running from a single ancient fuse! And last, but not least, all windows and doors had been replaced with double-glazed units, making the house much warmer in winter.

So, would we achieve our goal of having an indoor bathroom during our second year of residency?

Technically, yes. Although as you can infer from the title of this book, we're not quite there yet!

Cast

The Diary Continues: April

HOT water is finally available on tap! We plant trees, fill the thermal store and install the boiler stove, and I construct a wood stove out of an old electric water heater.

We visited neighbour J, taking the newly-purchased trailer with us. The reason for this was that she'd offered us a couple of young plum trees which had sprouted underneath their parent. We ended up with five fairly decent young trees; and four elder saplings as well. All of these have now been planted either in the garden around the pond, or along the fence line. Actually later in the year when their leaves emerged, we discovered that the plums were actually cherries; as they have two bright red nodules at the base of each leaf. A happy mistake, as cherries are even better than plums in our opinion!

We also took the opportunity of inspecting the elder trees we'd planted last year, and we were pleased to find that they have all survived the winter and have started sprouting new leaves. Unfortunately it will be several years before we can enjoy elderflower champagne and elderberry wine from our own trees. I suspect a lot of home-brewing will take place this year.

The thing is, we will need to make the most of the fruits and berries when they are in season; and it's to our advantage to have a stock of different wines and beers in store for when friends come around to visit. It will save us a fortune as well, as we won't have to buy any wine or beer. Besides, I enjoy making country wines. And beer, of course! We do have an apéritif in the evenings; but after all we are in France...

LSS did some fishing in the pond, catching 49 gudgeon in under an hour, so we had a fry-up that evening. I think she used a grand total of two earthworms as bait. There are lots of carp in the pond as well; but I've found that these taste a bit muddy. We'll probably need to rescue another old bathtub from the Aged FIL's field and fill it with rainwater. If we put any carp we catch in that water for a day or so, hopefully that will purge some of the muddy taste. I suspect I may have to rig up some sort of aeration mechanism to keep the fish happy for their final hours though.

The trailer has been used to visit the local quarry 15km away. We came back with 700kg of 8/16 gravel. I used half of it as hardcore for the floor of one of the little rooms next to the workshop; this room will be used for storage, but we need a solid floor first. The layer of compacted gravel will be covered with a lime concrete floor. Unfortunately it's not warm enough yet to pour concrete, so the tractor-powered concrete mixer is still in the Aged FIL's barn; we may bring it to La Darnoire once the weather warms up. Or maybe not. It doesn't have a tilting mechanism for the drum; one has to use the levers inside the tractor cab for that. Which I suspect will be a bit of an annoyance – we may end up buying an electric one instead.

The project for providing the house with hot water is nearly finished. We chose to use a thermal store rather than an electric hot-water cylinder. The thermal store is a 500-litre galvanized steel tank which was donated to us by our neighbours T&M. It is situated on the upper floor of this two-storey farmhouse, and is connected with two 22mm copper pipes to the boiler stove in the room below. It contains three coils of 16mm copper pipe; the upper coil provides domestic hot water; the middle coil provides hot water to a radiator in the bedroom; and the lower coil will be connected to a home-made solar thermal panel on the roof, which will transfer heat from the sun into the tank.

The thermal store was filled in stages. Unfortunately when it was three-quarters full I noticed a leak where the topmost copper coil exits the cylinder, so I had to drain some of the water off again. Once the connection dried out, I temporarily resolved the leak by using some silicone sealant, as we had already returned the oxy-acetylene brazing torch which was borrowed from JP. The leak was later permanently repaired by using some JB WaterWeld – a type of epoxy – designed for marine repairs. It is unaffected by water.

In the lounge below the thermal store, I enlarged the current hole in the lounge ceiling to take the larger 139mm diameter stovepipe of the boiler stove. The old stovepipe from the previously scrapped wood-burner was 100mm in diameter. I then used lime mortar to seal around the edges of the hole. Plastering upside-down is probably one of my least favourite jobs in the entire world. Lime mortar went all over the place including up my sleeves (or I should say down my sleeves as my arms were in an upright position.)

We had to purchase another three metres of stovepipe, because the boiler stove is on one side of the room, and the stovepipe exit is in the ceiling on the opposite side of the room. The boiler stove had to be positioned where it is because the thermal store is directly above it. It looks very odd to have a great big stainless steel pipe running across the lounge just below the ceiling!

But we finally have HOT WATER on tap.

For readers accustomed to the standards of modern living, it may be difficult to comprehend just how much of a game-changing event this has been. Hot water from a tap is something which most people take for granted. But just imagine for a moment that your hot water cylinder is out of action, and the only method you have for heating water is in a saucepan on the stove. Forget about having a nice hot shower! The most you can hope for is a warm bath; which takes absolutely ages to prepare. But having hot water at the turn of a tap – ooh, such luxury! I installed a temperature probe in the top of the thermal store, at the level at which the water enters the tank from the boiler stove, and ran a wire through the ceiling to a digital temperature gauge. I didn't even have to drill a hole through the ceiling; I just re-used an existing hole which was originally used for the cable of a television aerial. This gauge is just a temporary measure; I will be making up a proper panel which will house 5 digital gauges:

- Temperature at top of tank

- Temperature at bottom of tank

- Temperature of hot water supply

- Temperature of solar panel outlet

- Room temperature upstairs

This morning (because even though the outside temperature had reached a balmy 9 °C it still felt cold) we put some paper and kindling in the boiler stove, lit the touch-paper, and stood back.

The stove took a while to get going, but we watched the temporary temperature gauge with fascination.

10h45: Stove lit. Temperature of water 13.1 °C

11h33: Now at 16.7 °C

11h55: 42.3 °C

12h02: 46.8 °C

12h13: The magical 50 °C

The temperature seems to have stabilized at around 51 °C. I estimate we have around 450 litres of water to heat up. Or, to be more exact, I should say, heat down. Because the hot water from the boiler stove enters at the top of the thermal store, and the cooler water from the bottom of the thermal store returns to the boiler. Anyway, at 12h30 we couldn't wait any longer, and turned on the hot tap. Well, I say hot tap. There is a tap, but it's a lever-type, at the end of a flexible hose. This is a temporary arrangement until such time as the kitchen sink is installed. However, this can now be used to fill the bathtub. Imagine our delight when hot water started flowing! We would now be able to have a bath without having to heat the water in large saucepans on the wood stove. Having piped hot water is definitely a first for this old house!

Whilst on the subject of woodstoves, I put the finishing touches to the manufacture of my steampunk-style electric hot water-cylinder workshop woodstove. Say that three times quickly!

You see, LSS had given me a propane space heater for my birthday several years ago; this was used quite a lot in my garage in the UK when I was rebuilding my Land Rover. Unfortunately when I connected it up here, I found that the thermocouple had expired. In other words, it would only function if you kept the ignition button depressed. Perhaps unsurprisingly, spares proved to be unavailable; so instead of spending money on another model, I decided to build myself a wood-burning stove.

Having found an old electric hot water cylinder in one of the barns at the Aged FIL's place, I decided to convert this into a wood burner. This cylinder had obviously been donated to the Aged FIL by some well-meaning person who had felt sorry for him, as he did not have a bathroom. Or indeed, any hot water on tap. Needless to say, it was never used.

The advantage of using an electric hot water cylinder is that the walls are fairly thick, which is useful if you're going to burn wood in it! As winter temperatures here can get very low indeed, this would make the difference between my simply staying in the house all winter, or using the workshop for making things.

The first job was to remove the external shell, and then scrape off the polystyrene insulation. Once this had been removed, I re-fitted the brackets. The cylinder was originally designed to be used horizontally, and these brackets would be ideal for fixing the stove to a supporting frame. I then removed the heating element and thermostat, and cut off the top of the cylinder by using an angle grinder. This top was then converted into a door by fabricating a couple of hinges. The larger hole left by the heating element was closed with a small piece of glass so that the status of the fire can be checked.

To provide a regulated airflow to the fire I installed a screw-type ceramic air vent taken from a small (scrapped) woodstove. This stove was originally in the lounge, but it fell to pieces when we moved it. I kept the air vent and door latch for re-use, but the rest of the stove went on to the scrap-metal pile.

For the stovepipe, I cut a hole in the side of the cylinder and welded on a piece of steel drainpipe. Coincidentally this was exactly the right size for some pieces of stovepipe which I also found in the Aged FIL's barn. I didn't bother doing anything fancy for the stovepipe; I just poked it through a convenient aperture in the workshop wall. The workshop used to be a stable; and there are four "ventilation" openings, two in each side wall. Of course these will eventually need to be sealed up if I want to keep any heat inside!

A stand was then fabricated; the scrap pile provided some pieces of angle-iron which had been bolted together to support some long-gone piece of equipment, and by adding a couple of cross-pieces cut from the support brackets of an old barn door, I had a frame which was just the right height!

As it was a rainy afternoon, I figured that I just HAD to test it. I'm pleased to report it works fine. The only downside is that we will soon have three wood-burning stoves at La Darnoire, which means some unfortunate person will need to cut a lot more wood. Oh. That would be me.

I also continued the maintenance work on my Honda Pan European ST1100 motorcycle; new tyres were installed, the wheels have now been re-fitted and new stainless steel brake lines installed. Whilst the front wheel was off I also changed the coolant, using more ecology-friendly propylene glycol instead of the usual ethylene glycol. Now I just need to bleed the front brakes and put the body panels back on.

LSS took advantage of some sunshine to use the motor-driven tiller on the garden, ploughing in the rabbit-dropping compost we brought back from the Aged FIL's farm. I suspect the first plants will soon be sown.

As my contribution to the gardening, I sprayed the four peach trees with a copper sulphate solution as the buds were about to break. Last year they suffered badly from peach leaf curl. As long as we don't get any unseasonal frost this year we may even get some fruit – unlike last year when we didn't get a single peach, pear or apple!

LSS harvested the remaining parsnips a couple of days ago and the next batch of parsnip wine is brewing. Nothing was wasted; once the parsnips had released their juice for the wine, LSS turned them into a parsnip lasagne. This is just like a normal lasagne but instead of using pasta, you use the sliced parsnips!

I've made a couple of racks to fit in our lightbulb-powered food dehydrator, so when our next crop of tomatoes is ready for harvest, we'll be ready to dry some.

Whilst on the subject of food, my mother used to have a recipe book from East Africa. One of the tried-and-tested recipes was for a chicken curry. Well, I was never able to get the dish to taste the same as the way Mum made it, until now. My sister mentioned that she had found this recipe book amongst my mother's effects, so I asked her to photocopy this page for me. We decided that last night would be Curry Night. And I was delighted to find that it tasted exactly like I remembered! The missing secret ingredient turned out to be the apricot jam.

We had the curry with little side dishes of coconut, peanuts, raisins, apple, grated carrot and grated parsnip. And of course rice. We'll consider doing it again in the near future, and this time we'll invite the neighbours around to try it. I suspect they will not have had curry like this before (even if they've had curry at all – because it's not that well-known in France.)

Mum's Curry Recipe (quoted verbatim from the book):
"Ingredients:
3 fair-sized onions
3 heaped tablespoons fat
2 tablespoons curry powder
2 tablespoons vinegar
1 cup gravy or soup
1 tablespoon good chutney
2 tablespoons milk

1 tablespoon apricot jam

Meat – fresh or cooked

Method:

Cut onions finely; brown in boiling hot fat; then add curry powder. Stir constantly, to prevent the powder burning, for ten minutes (this prevents the raw taste that is sometimes found in curries when the powder is not well cooked). Add gravy or soup – if neither is available use the same quantity of hot water; cook for five minutes; stir constantly, then add chutney, apricot jam, vinegar, and a little sugar. When the curry is suited to taste, add milk; cook all together for 10 minutes, then put in the meat, cut up in small pieces, and allow the curry to simmer on the edge of the fire[1] till required for the table. The longer the curry simmers the better it is, but care must be taken not to let it burn.

If fresh meat is used for the curry, the meat must be fried till half cooked before it is added to the curry gravy. Just before serving the curry, add one tablespoon of milk; this gives the curry a soft taste which all good curries ought to have. If coconut milk is to be had, it is better than fresh milk."

We also visited a restaurant in Salbris with LSS's three cousins. Since they learned that we were now in France they instituted an annual Easter get-together. I wasn't looking forward to it much, as they all talk nineteen to the dozen, generally all at the same time. Still, it's only once a year.

---

[1]Note that this recipe book dates from the 1950's and was very much aimed at a non-urban lifestyle. Other recipes involved using cleaned empty petrol tins as cooking vessels. Nowadays, of course, we have saucepans.

Towards the end of the month, the weather turned cold again, and we had a few flurries of snow. It's supposed to be spring!

We have had our first experience with a delivery company called GLS. I think this is an acronym for Goods-Losing Service. I had purchased a USB car radio head unit on the 8th from Ebay, with the intention of upgrading the audio system on my motorcycle. The seller had despatched the item using UK's Parcel Force. It transpires that Parcel Force gives the package to their French counterpart, called GLS. On the 10th of April I received an email from GLS saying that delivery was scheduled for the 11th. Well, the 11th came and went, and no parcel arrived. I then received another email from GLS saying that they could not deliver the parcel, because the address was incomplete. Well, it wasn't. Mind you, it is the shortest address I've ever had. It's simply name-of-farm, name-of-village, postcode.

It took a lot of email correspondence and another week before the parcel was finally delivered. I can only hope we never have dealings with GLS again.[2]

Some bricklaying has also taken place. I've been constructing a small supporting wall in the kitchen, for the new worktop. I've also moved forward with the copper piping for the kitchen sink taps. Once the new sink is in place we won't have to

---

[2]This was a rather vain hope. We order lots of things online, and GLS seems to be the courier of choice around here, especially for larger items. However, more conscientious drivers are able to find us without any trouble.

crouch down to do the washing up (LSS's grandparents were considerably shorter than people are today).

May

Problems with chimneys occur and are resolved. The road past the house is finally repaired by the village contractor. Kitchen renovations take place, and a composting area is constructed.

I was kept exceedingly busy once again, resolving sundry issues.

The first problem which had to be resolved was with the new boiler stove. Well, actually, it wasn't the boiler stove itself. Everything worked fine for a week, but one particularly overcast and rainy afternoon I opened the bedroom door to find that the room was full of smoke. There was no smoke near the stove, none in any of the other two rooms, and the stovepipe and chimney seemed to be leak-free as well.

When LSS arrived home after having given an English class (did I mention she now teaches English to individuals?) we investigated.

By peering through a cleanout hatch in the chimney upstairs with the aid of a torch, I found that some bricks had dropped down inside the chimney at the level of the upstairs floor. This exposed the air space between the loft floor and the ceiling of the living room. Smoke was entering into this air space, drawn by the extractor fan vent in the bedroom, and the only way out was between the beams supporting the bedroom ceiling.

I should perhaps mention that the reason we have an extractor fan vent in the bedroom is because this is an old house. It was built in 1880, and at that time there were no damp-proof membranes. This is not normally a problem, because the lime mortar used in the original construction enabled the walls to "breathe". However, a later owner decided to take advantage of modern technology; namely Portland cement. The outside walls were rendered with this stuff up to the level of the windows. And the internal walls were rendered with it entirely, from floor to ceiling.

The walls are therefore unable to breathe and as a result, we have a problem with damp and mould. The only viable short-term solution was to improve ventilation; hence the addition of an extractor fan (called a VMC here – short for *Ventilation Mécanique Contrôlée*), with vents in the pantry and bedroom.

I have therefore had to spend time dismantling part of the upstairs chimney in order to create a hole into which I could crawl, in order to access the inside of the chimney to repair the dropped bricks using lime mortar. Then once that was done, I had to replace the bricks which I had removed to create the hole. Not much fun at all really. It's a good thing I'm not claustrophobic.

For the thermal store, I purchased some Fernox Central Heating protector. As the water simply thermo-syphons between the store and the boiler stove, I thought it would be a good idea to add some form of rust-protection. I'm not too sure whether the Fernox has had any effect though; the water still looks rusty.

Another event which occurred was that the local village contractor turned up to repair the road running past our driveway. He and LSS were at school together. Well, it is a small village, so everybody knows everybody!

Although it is a public road, albeit unpaved, it had fallen into disrepair because nobody had lived here for years; the village was not going to spend money on maintaining a road which was not being used. So whenever it rained, it became a sea of mud. Last year LSS had pointed this out to the mayor, and he had promised he would take care of it.

Well, the road renovation did not go smoothly. On the first day the contractor spread a layer of building rubble/landfill. That evening we strolled along the road removing bits of plastic bags, electrical wiring, sharp pieces of metal, and sundry other rubbish. The following day a layer of pond mud was laid down. It must have been pond mud because the smell was unmistakeable. Of course the day after this, it rained. And the resultant muddy soup had to be seen to be believed. Tractors or Land Rovers would possibly have been able to get through, but we couldn't. And unfortunately the state of the road is the direct cause of the ST1100 languishing in the garage. It's all very well having a touring motorcycle, but if one can't get it onto a tarmac road there's not much point in having it!

Fortunately we have an escape route via the Aged FIL's farm, so LSS went to see the mayor to complain that the road was now in an even worse state than it was before the work started. A few more days went by, and another layer of stuff was added to the mud; some grey clay chippings. With the aid of the increasingly rare sunshine, this dried out the part of the road in front of our driveway; but further away it's still very soft and squishy. Fortunately the muddy soup had been seen by the councillor in charge of roads (and his son is currently benefiting from LSS's English lessons - small world!) so we have been promised that further material will be added to the remaining squishy bits. We live in hope.

We managed to find some more pallets and I have now started constructing a composting area which will consist of four "compartments" with the walls being made from recycled pallets. This in itself has been an issue; because the rare pallets we are able to find are not exactly perfect. The nicely square solid ones are all "consigned" which means they are destined to be returned to the delivery company. In other words we end up with the odd-sized ones which nobody else wants. Still, at least they're free, so I shouldn't complain. It just means I need to add more slats of wood in order to create pallets of uniform size. And the little half- and quarter-pallets will come in handy too; I will cut the slats into uniform lengths and make them into shingles for the future porch over the kitchen door.

Some bad news is that it looks like my bonsai trees have died, with the exception of two pines. It was obviously too warm and dry inside the house this winter. But if we'd left them outside they would probably have frozen solid anyway. Pity.

The kitchen is now starting to take shape. The old kitchen sink was removed, and I used my rotary hammer to take the old tiles off the wall. These appeared to be stuck in place with high-powered industrial concrete, instead of tile adhesive, and I'm not joking. I've also finished the supporting wall for the worktop. Now I need to fabricate some more copper pipe connections and the waste water connections, and the new kitchen sink can go in. I also need to use the router on one edge/end of each of the two pieces of worktop so that they form an "L" shape. In the interim, we're washing up in a plastic bowl supported on a plank between two trestles. We do have a dishwasher, but there's no way to connect it up yet!

At least the gas cooker is now back in the kitchen instead of being in the living room, and I've drilled a hole through the kitchen wall for the gas supply pipe. There won't be enough room for the gas cylinder in the kitchen, so it will have to go outside. This in turn means I need to build an outside "cupboard" for it. So I'm considering dividing this cupboard into two sections with the upper section being used to store some firewood. Which means I then need to make a hatchway through the kitchen wall so that the wood can be accessed. Oh there's no end to the fun! Still, this will free up even more room in the kitchen as we can then get rid of the wood-box (which is a home-made cupboard constructed from what looks like the shell of an old kitchen range). Full marks to the Aged FIL for recycling.

By the end of the month, the kitchen counter tops were cut to size and installed, and the plumbing under the new sink had been completed. So the dishwasher finally came out of the barn and into the kitchen. However, we can't use it yet because we can't find the rinse-aid anywhere!

The kitchen wastewater pipe simply drains into a 20-litre bucket at the moment, which I empty every morning. This is obviously a temporary arrangement until the reedbed is up and running. As the house is not connected to mains drainage (and neither is there a septic tank) we will need to install some means of treating grey water. The most ecological method for achieving this will be the construction of a reedbed. I'm not too sure how previous occupants of this house washed; but I suspect they used a bucket and facecloth, and then simply emptied the bucket into the garden. As we have a composting toilet, the only waste water the house produces is termed "grey" water, coming from baths, showers, or the kitchen sink. A reedbed is able to clean this grey water prior to it re-entering the environment.

I also moved the washing machine from the barn. I should perhaps mention here that what we refer to as the "barn" is not a separate building. It is a continuation of the house itself. There is no interconnecting door though; to access it one has to go outside and enter through a pair of large decrepit wooden doors. The house itself consists of three rooms (four if you include the tiny "pantry"). A kitchen, a large bedroom, and a slightly smaller room which we are using as a lounge or living room. The plan is to steal some space from the bedroom to create a corridor, then break through the end wall, thus providing internal access to the "barn". The future bathroom will then be constructed here, once the barn area has been renovated. At the moment it is just a large open area with a dirt floor, no ceiling, and full of cardboard boxes from our house move. There is an unobstructed view of the rafters and roof tiles. It's somewhat draughty in there.

The washing machine has now been moved onto a pallet-wood base in the outbuilding housing the old "*ballon*" (pressured water storage vessel fed from the well) as this is currently the only viable place for it. I connected up a water supply from the kitchen using the old underground pipe which used to feed the kitchen tap from the well water. The only problem with this is that there is a lot of sludge and rust in the old steel pipe even though it's been flushed through a few times, so before we can use the washing machine I need to get and install another water filter. I can see another trip to BricoDepot in Orleans is on the cards. The waste water from the washing machine will exit via a plastic pipe into the field next to the chickens. This is again a temporary measure until the reedbed is up and running.

And although there is an electricity outlet there, it's an ancient plug socket. Renovating this is also on my "To Do" list but in the interim I ran a piece of galvanized catenary wire between the house and the outbuilding, at a height of some 3.5 metres above the ground. This provided the support for a length of PVC-insulated electrical wire which runs from the circuit breaker panel in the house to a modern plug socket I installed in the outbuilding.

Despite the rainy weather, LSS cut the grass in the borehole field with the tractor – this was necessary as the grass was nearly chest height and could have hidden any number of wild animals.

I cut some overhanging branches on the road between the

two farmhouses, so the road is once again passable for ordinary vehicles.

The garden isn't doing very much at the moment, again probably due to the cool cloudy weather. I'm starting to get sunshine withdrawal symptoms!

Wildlife diary: Mrs. Duck had returned to the pond, and constructed a nest at the base of one of the willow trees, containing 13 eggs. We have kept an eye out for foxes; last year a vixen had constructed a den not 50 metres from the garden fence. We've kept a regular check on this area and it looks like she has not returned this year. By the end of the month we had eleven little ducklings following their mother around the pond; a more successful outcome than last year!

June

FOUNDATION work for the barn is carried out. The washing machine is operational, and the workshop and garage get gutters. The compost enclosure is completed, and we test the quality of a Victorinox Swiss army knife.

Ooh, sunshine! For the second day running. Finally we are getting some much-needed Vitamin D.

LSS is an even happier bunny now – the washing machine is finally up and running, so she no longer has to go down to the river and bash the clothes on a flat rock. No, just kidding. We have been using the Aged FIL's washing machine since we arrived here.

I have now completed the guttering for the workshop and garage, so at least now we don't get dripped on when opening the doors when it's raining. I need to lead the workshop rainwater away to the closest ditch, which will involve laying pipe in a trench about thirty metres in length. I spied a ditch-digging attachment for the tractor in a shed at the Aged FIL, so we'll need to connect it up and see if it still works.

I carried on tackling the fallen oak tree at the Aged FIL's house, cutting it into firewood- sized logs with the chainsaw. The logs were then split and stacked in the wood store; I've started the second tier now.

Last Saturday we were able to recuperate a trailer-load of pallets, so these were used to finish the construction of the composting area, and to start the second woodshed. The base of this additional shed is complete, as is the first course of the walls. I think another six pallets should do the job.

My sister had suggested a money-making idea we could try; growing truffles. However, I did some research and it doesn't look like it will work here. I believe somebody in the area tried it unsuccessfully a couple of years ago; apparently the soil here is of the wrong type. Although one can buy truffle-inoculated trees, we would need to set aside an area of land first in which to plant them. Then it would be a matter of fencing off the area with an electric fence. There are a lot of wild boars in the area and they love truffles even more than humans do. So I don't think it's really feasible.

My "To Do" list just seems to get longer, no matter how many items are ticked off. At times I feel like I'm trying to push a large collection of boulders uphill all at once. It does get a bit disheartening; but suddenly one arrives at a point where several mini-projects reach their completion, and there is a real sense of achievement. My philosophy is simple; fill each day as productively as possible; it doesn't matter which particular project is moved forward as long as time is not wasted. But that's not to say I don't enjoy a ten-minute break now and then! One or two of LSS's adult pupils have expressed admiration for her gardening prowess. "Oh, I'd like to do that. But I just don't have the time."

"We all have twenty four hours in the day," she replied. "It depends on how you choose to spend them."

If you're happy to waste time by sitting in front of the television for several hours every day, you shouldn't really complain. We're so glad we no longer have a television.

We had our first strawberries of the year; the recent sunshine was just what they had been waiting for. As they are growing in such profusion, I suspect we'll be having some every day for the foreseeable future! I may try drying some, which reminds me – I still haven't made a solar food dryer.

Our current apparatus for food dehydration consists of a galvanized metal garden incinerator. This is like a large dustbin, except it has lots of holes in it. I installed a 60W lightbulb in the base, and a couple of wire mesh racks near the top. The lightbulb is of the ordinary incandescent type; this is important because this sort of bulb emits more heat than it does light. It wouldn't work with a fluorescent or LED bulb. The heat causes air to rise up past the food to be dried, carrying any moisture with it. It works very well, but we would really like a method which does not use any electricity.

We have, however, commenced another method of food storage. It's a German recipe called a *Rumtopf*. Basically you take an earthenware storage jar, and as fruits become available throughout the year, they are added to the jar. The layer of fruit is sprinkled with sugar, and then the whole lot is covered with rum. You keep adding layers of fruit, sugar, and rum until the jar is full, and then have it as a Christmas dessert. We'll see if it's any good.

I retrieved a heavy steel frame from the Aged FIL's pile of scrap. I intend putting it to good use as an apple cider press frame, using a hydraulic car jack to apply pressure. I had previously made a similar cider press when we lived in Britain, constructing it out of several layers of marine plywood according to a diagram I'd found on the Internet.

Unfortunately it was not up to the job and cracked. As the Mark II model will be made of steel girders, this should not be an issue! It's not going to be much fun moving it around though, so I may have to decide on a permanent location for it.

The home-made apple scratter is still in working order, so crushing the fruit should not be a problem. There are quite a few feral apple trees scattered around the property, and this year the blossoms are in profusion; probably the trees are trying to make up for last year's late frost which killed every single one.

The pear tree in the garden is also making good progress and as long as nothing unforeseen occurs we can look forward to a bumper crop of edible pears as well. There are some pear trees at the Aged FIL's property as well, but these are apparently not very nice to eat. I think some perry manufacturing may well be on the cards!

Speaking of making alcoholic beverages, we visited Neighbour J. She had telephoned to inform us that all her elder trees were in full flower. Half an hour's labour saw us with several plastic bags full of the flowers. April's batch of parsnip wine has been bottled, and as we are missing the comforting "plop-plop" caused by the airlock of the fermenting bucket in the corner of the kitchen, a new batch of elderflower champagne is on the agenda. LSS will also be making some elderflower cordial. This year should also see us attempting blackberry wine. Not that we drink a lot mind you. But we'll have to start, because we need more empty bottles...

Repairs have started on the northern exterior wall of the house. The lowest courses of bricks have spalled (cracked) due to earth having been piled up against the wall. The lack of gutters – and no proper drainage until now – meant that this earth absorbed a lot of water, which made its way into the brickwork. During winters, the freezing temperatures caused the bricks to deteriorate. I am removing the bricks one small section at a time, and creating a limecrete foundation. Once this has set, I can start replacing the bricks. I also made a limecrete foundation for a small rainwater butt near the kitchen as I'm fed up with straightening the subsiding bricks upon which it currently rests. Blooming moles! Mixing limecrete in a wheelbarrow with a shovel is not fun. (Yes, there is a tractor-powered cement mixer at the other property but it's too much of a mission to fetch it!)

Limecrete, by the way, is simply concrete made by mixing hydraulic lime, sand, aggregate, and water. There is no Portland cement in the mix. The advantage of limecrete over concrete is that it breathes, and is more flexible; so there is no need for expansion joints or waterproof membranes.

Oh dear. LSS has experienced some misfortune. We had both gone to the Aged FIL's house; LSS had to sort out some of the Aged FIL's paperwork, and I was collecting bits of wood which could be taken back to our house and cut up for firewood. LSS finished before me, so decided to take the tractor with the brushcutter attachment back to our house and cut some of the grass in the alleyways ready for this season's hunting. I gave her my key ring containing the house keys.

I should explain at this point that there are only a few keys on my key ring; namely for the house back door, post-box, workshop, and my motorcycle top box. Also on the key ring is my sharp, well-used, trusty Swiss army knife. I also need to mention that the tractor is fairly old, and has several gaps in the floorboards, especially at the front underneath the pedals. (Can you see where this is going?)

After an hour or so, it was approaching lunchtime, so I finished up at the Aged FIL and went back to our house, where LSS had just finished the morning's session with the tractor.

"Right, let's have lunch," she said.

"Good idea," I replied.

"Well, go on then, open the door."

"Eh? I don't have the keys. I gave them to you. Don't tell me you've lost them!"

"Oh yes, so you did. I put them... er... uh oh."

"What do you mean, 'uh oh'?"

"Well, I don't have pockets. So I put them on the dashboard of the tractor. But they're not there now!"

We looked in the cab of the tractor. No keys.

"They must have fallen off the dashboard onto the floor."

"Yes. And unfortunately they're not on the floor now. They probably went through one of these holes."

Fortunately the spare keys to the front door of the house were hanging up on a hook in the kitchen. I found a 5-metre length of rigid plastic tube, and with LSS peering through the kitchen window and calling instructions - "Up a bit! To the left! Go in a bit more! Now down a bit! You're nearly there! Go right! Down a bit!" I was able to guide the plastic tube through the cat flap and dislodge the keys from the hook on the wall. Once they were on the floor it took several more minutes of manoeuvring before I was finally able to reach through the cat flap with my arm and grab them.

Having once again gained access to the house, I fetched my metal detector, and started walking up and down over the freshly-cut grass.

It didn't take long before I heard the high-pitched whine through my headphones. Now Victorinox make very good knives. But they're not designed to go through the whirling heavy steel blades of a tractor brush-cutting attachment. Smashed is not the word. And as for the keys: I found lots of small pieces of metal. But even with the best glue in the world there was no way to piece them back together. The only one I found undamaged was the one for the motorcycle top box. Fortunately we had spares for all the others. We now keep a spare back door key in a secret location in the farmyard!

And LSS bought me a new Swiss army knife. So all's well that ends well...

Wildlife diary: The ducklings have now doubled in size. As you can imagine they don't let us get too close so taking any photos are difficult. They also don't keep still long enough for us to be able to count them; we think we still have eleven. LSS bought some wild duck food and we've put a small bowl near the pond. The ducklings simply climb into the bowl and scoff away to their hearts' content, and Mrs. Duck has a good few beakfuls as well! Apparently it takes up to three months before they are ready to fly, so it looks like we'll have the pleasure of their company for a while yet.

July

O NCE the chicken shed and coop are constructed, we get some hens. Ditch-digging for the horse paddock commences, and we go fishing in the canal.

One of LSS's cousins paid us a visit; and also went to visit the Aged FIL. The work which I had done around the house was duly inspected, although there was again puzzlement over why we wanted to heat water without using the abundant supply of electricity generated from France's 59 (at the time of writing) nuclear power stations. Even when we pointed out that heating water with wood fuel (and later solar power) would save us money on electricity, I think she still considers us to be fruitcakes.

We have decided we will get some hens. Not only will this make us self-sufficient as far as eggs are concerned, but they can also dispose of what little kitchen waste we have. The remainder will, of course, go into the compost.

To this end, I have been constructing a chicken shed. Next to the outbuilding comprising the garage and a storage room is an open-fronted corrugated-iron-roofed structure which LSS's grandmother originally used for doing the laundry. The Aged FIL had been using it to store rubbish; old broken ceramic pots, empty medicine bottles, and spools of rusty barbed wire, just to mention a few items. Once this had all been cleaned out, I enclosed the front by re-using some corrugated iron panels scavenged from the Aged FIL's farm, and also installed a door. That takes care of the roosting area. The next step is to build them a run. But before doing this, I need to dig a trench and install some conduit to carry water from our borehole to the field which we're considering using for a horse paddock. This conduit runs underneath the planned location of the chicken run, so it makes sense to install this first!

Horses? Yes, as though I don't have sufficient things to occupy my time, we've come up with another item for the To Do list. We have – or should I say LSS has – discovered that the closest town, Lamotte Beuvron, is the third largest equestrian centre in the world. Every summer there are quite literally thousands of horses attending competitions, and during this time their owners look for accommodation both for themselves and for their horses. Some are forced to stable their equine companions as far away as Orleans. At the moment it's just a national competition, but we've heard through the grapevine that it will very soon become an international one.

So, as we have the space, our bright idea is that next year we'll put an electric fence around one of the large fields on the property, and rent the space to horses. Or, to be more accurate, to their owners. This is known as grass livery; we provide the field, and water; but the feeding and care of the animals remains the responsibility of the owner.

So I started work on the digging. The end result was a shallow trench housing a corrugated plastic pipe containing a length of hosepipe, and an electrical cable which will carry the current for the electric fence.

Once the trench had been backfilled, I could build the chicken run. Having had some recent practice with the spade, I dug a new trench about 30cm deep around the perimeter of the planned run. Wooden posts were then sunk into the ground at each corner, and at regular intervals. More corrugated iron panels were then placed into the trench and screwed to the wooden posts before the trench was refilled. This design should ensure that the hens are safe from foxes trying to dig their way in.

I then fixed some chicken wire fencing to the top of the corrugated iron panels, so the end result was a stout barrier approximately six feet in height.

On the 14th July – a major public holiday in France – we went to a nearby town called Aubigny with T&M. It's the only place in France which still celebrates the close links between France and Scotland, the "Auld Alliance". It's known as the "City of the Stuarts". There was the obligatory parade, with lots of Scots pipe bands in kilts. Disappointingly though, I did not hear one Scots accent; all the participants appeared to be French!

Following a hastily-grabbed lunch and beer, we had a brief look at Mary Stuart's castle in the town centre; unfortunately only from the outside as it did not appear to be open to visitors. The village fairground proved to be more interesting; among the exhibitors were some blacksmiths happily hammering glowing red iron into fantastic shapes on their anvils. There was also a display of mediaeval jousting; although due to our late arrival we were at the back, and could only just make out the helmets and lances of the combatants over the heads of the crowd. On the way home from Aubigny we passed through another village, Souvigny-en-Sologne (not to be confused with the similarly-named Souvigny, which is in another region altogether). On the main residential street near the village church we saw a pile of bric-a-brac on the pavement, so stopped to have a look. It turned out that one of the houses had been converted into a junk shop. Well, the owners refer to it as an "antique shop" but in my opinion it was just a lot of rather old junk. The thing is: the owners still live in the house, so it was unclear whether an item was actually for sale, or part of the normal household equipment. For example: on the kitchen table amidst sets of mismatched wine-glasses and several piles of dust-collecting cutlery, was a plate of half-finished lunch. Even more surprising was the kitchen counter, home to a roosting hen – together with the obligatory droppings.

The front room housed an enormous doorless cupboard; complete with hanging clothes, all with price tags. The problem here was that a colony of insects appeared to have moved in; as the majority of the garments were rather moth-eaten.

The outside area was not much better; the back garden was fairly difficult to navigate. Old bedsteads jostled for room against broken watering-cans, piles of old roof-tiles, and stacks of used guttering. More hens were scratching forlornly amongst the remains of several dozen broken wooden chairs – obviously antiques, ha! - and a couple of geese honked angrily at us. We left in a rather bemused state, not having bought anything, much to the disappointment of the owners.

The kitchen cooker ran out of gas for the first time. This was not an issue; as I used to be a Boy Scout I was Properly Prepared and had a spare gas cylinder. However, this one is now propane, instead of butane. Why? Well, since the new installation of the kitchen sink and dishwasher took place, there was no room in the kitchen for the gas cylinder. It was therefore placed outside in a makeshift cupboard constructed from some small pallets, and covered with off-cuts of corrugated iron. This worked very well – until the outside temperature dropped. Butane cannot cope very well with lower temperatures; the gas is unable to vaporize properly. Propane, on the other hand, is meant for outdoor use. So if you intend to store your gas cylinder outside, propane is the gas to use. It functions just as well as butane. Of course this also meant that I now had to change the jets on the gas stove itself.

As the weather was fairly pleasant we took a Sunday off, and went down to T&M's house. They live approximately 100m from the Canal de la Sauldre, so we all went fishing. Construction of the canal started in 1848, and it was completed in 1869. The intention was to use it to transport fertilizer, and up to the year 1900 the barges were pulled along by manpower. Horses then took over until the canal closed in 1926. There are several species of fish in the water; and we caught several small catfish. By law these are not allowed to be returned to the water, as they are an invasive species, so we took them home for a fry-up. We found them much better eating than carp.

Construction of a porch over the kitchen door commenced. Because this door is in the end wall of the house, it is not protected from the elements; and kitty's cat-flap tends to get wet when it rains! During our last visit to Castorama (a DIY superstore) we saw a porch frame on sale for a very reasonable price, so we bought it. It's just a frame; it still needs roofing material to be added. I had considered tiles, but these would have been too heavy. Instead I calculated that wooden shingles would do the job. Of course finding these ready-made proved impossible. Undaunted, I looked to another source of wood; namely pallets. I already have several of these dismantled, and have started cutting the planks into suitable lengths.

Back to the poultry project...

With the main chicken coop completed, I constructed some nesting boxes and a roosting area in the chicken shed. For the nesting boxes I placed two pallets on end and joined them together with a third, which happened to have a solid top. This formed a sort of table. Then I fixed four wooden fruit crates to the top, and filled these with hay.

The roost was constructed using two poles which I leaned up against the back wall of the chicken shed. Some hazel branches were then placed across these two poles and tied in place with wire, forming a sort of ladder. The entire thing was then fixed to the wall using a convenient metal bracket which was already in place. I made a similar ladder construction to enable the hens to reach the nest-boxes.

It is important that the roosting height is greater than that of the nest-boxes; otherwise the hens will simply sleep in the nests. And as they tend to produce the most droppings during their sleeping period, this would mean the nests would rapidly get filthy.

The floor of the chicken shed consists of clay tiles. Under

the roost I placed a layer of straw, which should assist in keeping the floor clean.

With the habitat complete, we finally collected four new family members, namely:

The chickens!

And less than four hours after introducing them to their new home, we already had two eggs! Unfortunately the birds haven't yet figured out what the nest-boxes are for, so the eggs were laid in the middle of the pen. I'm sure they'll get the hang of it eventually.

And they also don't know how to roost. When we went out at dusk to shut them in, we found all four huddled together in a pile in a corner of the pen. Following some research, we've learned that the way to train them to roost is to wait until they've settled down for the night, then simply pick them up and put them onto their perch. Apparently they soon get the idea.

August

U SED tyres help with the pond erosion. Digging starts for the greywater reedbed, and a solar shower is constructed. More home brewing takes place, and the tractor suffers a puncture.

With the temperature starting to decrease, I have been busy trying to finish off a few smaller projects before the winter really starts to take hold.

Over the past couple of weeks I've been repairing some of the erosion in the pond. We fetched a trailer-load of old car tyres from the garage in the village. They were very happy to get rid of them. The tyres are placed horizontally against the eroded bank, filled with rubble, and then the next tier are laid on top. The final covering is clay and soil, which should enable grass and reeds to take root and stabilize the bank.

I've also excavated the trench which will contain a buried pipe to take run-off rainwater from the workshop roof to a drainage ditch about 30m away. Rainwater from the house roof goes into the six 510-litre drums for use in the garden; but rainwater from the workshop roof needs to go somewhere else. But of course it goes without saying that I also had to install rainwater guttering to the workshop roof. Hopefully this will ensure the workshop and contents become a bit drier. Before the guttering was installed, rainwater simply ran off the roof into the ground at the base of the walls. And due to the damp, all my tools are turning rusty.

The digging of the reedbed has also started. The site for the reedbed was marked out with metal poles, and I made a start at excavating the hole, but then LSS took over the shovel whenever she had a spare minute. The reedbed will treat the greywater from the house, cleaning it before it goes into the pond. It's simply a hole 2 metres wide by 5 metres long, half a metre deep, which will be lined with a PVC sheet and then filled with gravel in which we will plant reeds. 12 tons of gravel has already been delivered, so there's a huge pile of stones just outside the garden fence. LSS and I took turns at going out and digging a few wheelbarrow loads of soil out of the hole every day. Once the hole was dug, the base was levelled. A geomembrane was laid down, followed by a PVC pond liner. The membrane is there to protect the pond liner from roots and burrowing moles (of which there are many). All the soil which came out of the excavation was put in a heap near the pond, where it is being used to repair the erosion of the banks. The gravel will all need to be moved via wheelbarrow into the reedbed. Mind you, the distance it needs to be moved is only around 20 meters. We can't plant any reeds until next spring though.

We took a break from our reedbed-hole-digging, and went for a picnic with our neighbours T&M. We had planned on going by bicycle to a spot about 12 km away. LSS obviously already had a bicycle, left over from her school days. As for me, I was a bit lacking in the bicycle department; but fortunately the late MIL earned a lot of supermarket shopping "points" which she had redeemed to get a unisex "mountain bike" which was never used. I dusted it off, oiled the chain, and managed to adjust the saddle to suit my height. There are another two bicycles rusting away in a corner of the Aged FIL's workshop, so I'm not short of spare parts.

T&M are a friendly couple, both divorced, and each has a young daughter from their previous marriage, aged 12 and 10 respectively. Remarkably the two girls look like sisters. Fortunately T speaks fairly good English which gives the language centre in my brain a bit of a break.

LSS's garden is now producing well; radishes, lettuce, beetroot, carrots, peas by the kilo, beans... and we're also having strawberries or raspberries for pudding most days! The blackberries are a bit slow this year so I think it will be another couple of weeks before they're ready – as I mentioned previously, I intend trying my hand at making blackberry wine.

Speaking of wine, I'm currently brewing some pea-pod wine which actually smells rather nice![3] The parsnip wine supposedly isn't ready to drink yet but there was a little bit left over after bottling, so we tasted it. I must say we're very impressed. It has an after-taste of whisky. And as we both like whisky, that's a bonus. I also have a batch of beer on the go which I made from malted barley and hops. Yes, I do have two fermenting vessels. The beer should be ready for bottling next week. The last batch I brewed ended up at around 9% ABV, and tasted very good. In a few weeks the elderberries will be ready for picking; so it will be time to make elderberry

---

[3]Actually when we later tasted it, it was horrible. We won't be doing it again.

wine. This has always been one of our favourites. LSS also makes a very good elderberry cordial.

T&M are starting to refer to La Darnoire as "The Brewery". I can't understand why.

I've finally finished cutting up the fallen oak tree at the other farmhouse. This was blown down by a small tornado last year (it also ripped off some of the roof tiles of the Aged FIL's house). One of the two woodsheds is now full, so that should be the supply for next year sorted out. This year's firewood is already seasoned; being lots of scrap wood collected from the Aged FIL's outbuildings.Although the Aged FIL does have a tractor-mounted log splitter, I was unable to use it successfully. It can crush a cardboard box quite well, but as soon as the blade encounters anything stronger it gives up. I suspect there is a hydraulic fault somewhere, but whether this fault lies with the tractor or the log splitter I have not yet had the time to determine.

We did wheel the Aged FIL out to the tractor in his wheelchair for him to have a look at the hydraulic connections, in case I had connected them up incorrectly. This was a waste of time, as he said he couldn't remember where they went. He was possibly just being bloody-minded. I therefore resorted to the old-fashioned method of splitting the logs with an axe.

I have also re-used some of the old hosepipes which were lying around. I estimate the total length of these to add up to around 400m. Well, I laid out a quarter of this length in coils on top of the corrugated iron woodshed roof, and connected it up to a shower fixed to a builders' trestle. We can now have an outside shower with solar-heated water. The other end of the hosepipe is obviously connected to a tap fed by the household water supply. The shower itself was donated to us by T&M, courtesy of T's uncle, who was renovating his bathroom and replacing everything. The only issue was that the main control knob was missing; so in its place I installed an ordinary bathroom mixer tap which I bought cheaply off Ebay. I modified the tap slightly, and now by selecting the "shower" lever on the tap, water is directed to the upper spray, whilst the "bath" selection diverts the water to a hand-held shower nozzle. My old army ponchos are coming in handy for a shower screen. The water is nice and warm after a day in the sun; but it doesn't stay warm for long so one has to be quick!

We've also applied to the Mairie for planning permission to install a solar panel on the house roof. The way that the French planning permission system works in this area is that if you do not hear from them by the end of a two-month period, this means permission has been granted. Bizarre, I know.

This solar panel will not be photovoltaic though; it will be a solar thermal panel. It will work in the same manner as the hosepipes on the woodshed roof: coils of copper tubing will collect heat energy from the sun to provide domestic hot water. The thing is – I've calculated that the best size for the panel will be 2.4m x 1.2m, so I've no idea how I'm going to get it up onto the roof! Unfortunately it's not going to be practical to build it in situ. We may need someone with a cherry-picker (one of those machines with a lifting platform on which you can stand).

I have now isolated the old electric circuits in the lounge so they are ready to be ripped out; once that's done I can finish the re-plastering and LSS can do the painting. We can then move our computer desks in from the barn, and once our computers are installed we won't be squabbling over who gets to use the laptop!

LSS's English lessons are on hold at the moment because her younger pupils have finished the school year, and the adult students are on holiday. She gets a bit frustrated at times because the students tend to ring up wanting to move their lessons to different times; or indeed different days. However, some good news is that she was approached by a training company, and has been awarded a contract to teach English for two full days per week to two classes of managers at a company with offices in Bourges and Selles Saint-Denis. At least those days are fixed and won't be moved around every five minutes.

This brings me to the subject of income, as I'm sure you were wondering how we're managing to pay the bills without my having a full-time job. Well, I do have a full-time job - fixing up this farmhouse! I just don't get a salary for it! We're extremely fortunate in that due to our self-sufficient lifestyle, our costs are minimal. And the biggest blessing is that we have no rent or mortgage to pay. Whatever money LSS earns covers our monthly living expenses. It's certainly less expensive to live here than in Britain.

Weather-wise it's been extremely hot recently with a couple of thunderstorms. Today is fairly grey and we're off to do the weekly shopping in Salbris. We tend to buy our fruit at the farmers' market now because we've found the supermarket fruit is: a) tasteless and b) spoils quickly. We obviously don't buy vegetables (except onions, which are cheaper to buy than to grow).

I had been using the late MIL's Renault 5 as a run-about on the farm, mainly for carrying wood. The fallen oak at the Aged FIL was transported piece by piece to the woodshed. The car wasn't really suited to the job, but the tractor had a puncture.

Again.

Fortunately it was one of the front wheels; I think the huge rear wheels would really need specialized equipment. When I owned a Land Rover, I had a farm jack which was very useful for changing tyres (it can also be used for winching, and pulling out fence posts, and all sorts of other little jobs!) I sold the Land Rover, but luckily kept the jack. This came in very handy for repairing the puncture on the tractor.

Once this was done, I mounted the transport box to the three-point mechanism at the back, and used that to ferry the rest of the wood. At present there are two woodsheds, and I'm hoping one will be sufficient for a winter's worth of supply. The temperature has been known to drop to as low as minus 20 degrees here at times.

We have been fishing with T&M a couple of times now along the canal. T was recently successful in catching a zander (also called a pike-perch) of about 40 cm in length. He cooked it for supper and invited us around to partake in the fishy feast. It wasn't too bad, but tasted a bit muddy. However, the meal was not improved by the fact that T&M had a heated argument with each other over the correct method of cooking the white sauce; so there was a bit of an atmosphere during dinner.

LSS and I have more luck in catching catfish; there are hundreds of them in the canal, and the ones we manage to catch are generally about 15cm long. They may be ugly, but they actually taste very nice, not at all muddy. There are also large carp in there, approximately 60cm in length (you can see them cruising up and down sometimes) but we're not that interested in catching them; we have carp in our pond and they DO taste muddy. One other species in the canal is perch. They're about the same size as the catfish, but are regrettably more difficult to catch, preferring lures. Again, not muddy-tasting.

Some of LSS's cousins visited us for a barbecue. There's one of them I don't particularly like, so I managed to avoid her as much as possible. Fortunately one of her sons speaks German so we managed to understand each other in mangled Teutonic and French. That was a bit of a wasted day though, showing them around, but LSS had been looking forward to it.

I have now finished the construction of the porch over the kitchen door. I installed the frame, which we had purchased, and then used installed the shingles which I had cut from some dismantled pallets. It's looking very rustic. The wood was painted with some old engine oil, which should help it to last longer. I didn't really want to use paint; which by the way is horrendously expensive in France.

The chickens are happy enough, producing an average of 3 eggs per day between the four of them. And we've also been looking after T&M's bunny rabbit while they're away for two weeks – we had to promise faithfully we wouldn't eat him.

The bottle store has also been completed. Sounds fancy, but it's simply a storage area in one of the outbuildings. I poured a lime concrete floor, installed shelving, and we now use this room to store all the glassware, for example empty bottles, jam jars, preserve jars etc.

In between all these little jobs I made a start on re-rendering the lounge walls so that LSS can get on with the painting. We've selected a sand-textured paint which should a) look rustic and b) hide any small imperfections. Once that's completed the computers can be set up.

A colour laser printer which we had ordered was delivered. LSS will need to be able to print in colour, as she will be giving English lessons at a company in Bourges next month. It will also come in handy for making her own business cards. Why a laser? Well, the cost of printing is less than that of an inkjet. And the price of laser printers has now reached very affordable levels.

The poor old ST1100 motorcycle has been languishing in the garage for ages. It's not that I don't want to ride it any more, it's just that I haven't really had time to take it out for a spin. Well, we were scheduled to visit Friend L for a lunch, and as the weather was fine, we decided to take the bike. She lives in a village called Bonny-sur-Loire, which is on the river Loire. Obviously. After lunch, we went for a walk along the river, and very picturesque it was too. The only disadvantage with taking the bike when visiting someone is that you have to take ordinary clothes along with you; it's not very practical going for a stroll wearing full leather motorcycle gear!

Wildlife diary: All eleven ducklings reached fledgling status exactly eight weeks after hatching. They flapped up and down the pond, practising take-offs. Eventually their wing muscles were strong enough and their Mum led them off on their maiden flight.

"Right you lot: full power on those wings, and remember what I told you about tail feathers."

(Chorus) "Yes Mum!" Zoom.

The next day there were once again eleven ducks in the pond; Mum had not returned with the youngsters. Their landing procedure has not quite been perfected yet.

Flapflapflapflapflapsplash.

They paddled around disconsolately for a day or two not quite knowing what to do, and eventually they flew off. Nine returned a few days later, but the numbers have now decreased and only six visit on a semi-daily basis. I reckon the others are a bit more adventurous, and have gone off to see the Big Wide World.

September

R EPAIRS are made to the foundations of the barn wall. Electrical renovation takes place in the lounge, and LSS teaches English in Bourges.

LSS has started giving English lessons to some staff in a company in Bourges. It turns out that she's required two days a week; and another four days a week are set aside for giving English lessons to individuals – both adults and school pupils. So I'm just getting on with things on my own. She still manages to find time for the garden, though! We have a fairly decent crop of beetroot at the moment. At least we're eating vegetables in season. One of these English lessons takes place one evening a week at a nearby castle. The student is the son of a very rich family who made their money in the sugar industry.

So this means that on this particular day it is my turn to cook dinner. One of these dinners was a Chinese stir-fry. Most of the vegetables were from the garden: green peppers, cabbage, and carrots. As a stir-fry is a last-minute event – excluding the preparation, of course – I lit the boiler stove and enjoyed the leaping orange flames, and watching the water temperature rise until LSS returned home.

A mega-brewing day took place. We now have 20 litres of elderberry wine bubbling away in the corner. We recently picked over 6kg of blackberries, so there is also a batch of blackberry wine on the go. Then we discovered another pear tree on the property, which has a lot of fruit. However, the pears are rather small and not very nice to eat, so we'll make perry out of these, and keep the nice pears from the tree in the garden for eating. This particular pear tree has been making up for the dearth of fruit last year, by producing buckets and buckets of pears. LSS has made several pear tarts, we now have pears for pudding most days, and I have the food dryer up and running with two trays of pear slices slowly desiccating. Once the elderberry and blackberry wines have finished fermenting, the production of perry will commence, using my newly-reconstructed cider press to squash the pulp. This will probably be followed by a batch of cider, as we have numerous feral apple trees scattered all over the property. The pea-pod wine has now been bottled. We had a taste, but it's still very green – in other words, acidic. Apparently it needs to be left for six months before it can be consumed. I don't have very high hopes for this one. Well, if it's no good, we can always use it in cooking![4]

We have also been recycling a lot of the old bottles which were lying abandoned in one of the outbuildings. The labels tend to soak off rather easily, as the bottles are at least 30 years old. Cleaning the inside is carried out by soaking with a solution of sodium percarbonate (which produces hydrogen peroxide, a sterilizing agent) and then scrubbing them with a bottle-brush. Yes, it's a lot of work but it saves us having to buy new bottles!

The lounge electrical work has finally been completed, and

---

[4]It wasn't. We did.

the re-plastering is well under way; I only have one wall left to do and then LSS can get busy painting.

The reedbed is now nearly filled with gravel. This will be in two layers; a coarse 10/20 stone to a depth of 40cm, and then a layer of pea gravel in which we can plant the reeds.

I have also finished excavating the soil next to the north wall of the house (in other words, the wall of the attached barn) to expose the crumbling brickwork, and have now repaired most of this. This particular excavation has left a shallow trench next to the wall. This will also be filled with gravel so that it acts like a French drain (rather apt, considering we're in France!) This gravel will also contain the greywater waste pipe leading to the reedbed, and the rainwater overflow pipe leading to the pond. Hopefully the gravel will provide some protection against frost. Digging is not finished yet, though - I still need to make a trench from the corner of the house to the reedbed so that the greywater pipe can be buried.

I've also poured a limecrete base for the future firewood cupboard which will eventually be accessible from inside the kitchen through a hatchway.

The hens have settled in very quickly; we've now trained them to roost on the proper hen-perch which I constructed instead of on the floor – obviously where they were raised, there were not such luxuries as proper perches. They've also been trained to drink from a suspended plastic 2-litre bottle, with a chicken watering nipple fitted. Sounds sexy, but isn't. The problem with giving water to chickens in a bowl is that the water becomes fowl (!) very quickly indeed. Egg production has been impressive – we've now had a total of 104 eggs. Obviously we don't eat them all ourselves; but our neighbours are happy to get farm-fresh eggs!

Hopefully this winter I'll be able to do some long-overdue work on the website, including uploading photos of the sundry renovation projects. We're looking forward to the completion of the lounge decorating, because then the computers can be extricated from their cardboard storage boxes.

As the weather has improved, I have been felling trees. Nothing major, just some thinning of oaks and birch which were encroaching onto the alleyway in the area we call "Piggy Corner". We gave it that name because the wild boar have dug a large wallow next to the boundary ditch. Other parts of the property have also been given names: like "Sloe Alley" - near the road leading to the house – obviously because there's an abundance of *Prunus spinosa*. And there's my particular favourite, "Soggy Bottom". Because it's not very well drained at all; it's at the bottom edge of the property, and if you sat down there that's what you'd get.

Towards the end of the month, LSS went to visit neighbour J, delivering some leafy vegetable scraps for her rabbits. LSS returned with not only a promise that next spring we would be given a live bunny (in order to start our own rabbit-rearing program), but also with a new addition to the family; a hedgehog we have named "Hubert". He has now taken up residence in the compost heap. Hopefully we can get a few more of these, as they are great at keeping the garden free from pests. Neighbour J said she'd keep an eye out for more – they tend to wander into her cow shed.

And as for the rabbits, a pair of bunny-skin moccasins will be on the drawing board...

One Sunday, we took the motorcycle to visit one of LSS's cousins on their farm in Chartres-sur-Cher. This is about 40km away. Unfortunately, all the menfolk of the household had gone hunting, and as the cousin-once-removed's girlfriend had just had a baby, everyone sat around in the dining room apparently discussing the care of infants; which LSS and myself found rather boring. Still, we had the motorcycle ride home to look forward to.

Apart from being kept busy with sundry construction work, the only thing preventing me from taking the bike out more often is where it's kept. The only vaguely suitable place is in the outbuilding we've decided to call the garage. However, there is no door. Well, there is a door, Jim, but not as we know it.[5] We're not too sure what the building was originally used for; but it last saw use as an apple-processing area. As well as the motorcycle, it currently contains an industrial-sized heavy cider press, and a 3-phase motor on a rotted timber frame. This motor is linked to a fearsome-looking apple grinder by way of a canvas belt. The Aged FIL blocked up the entrance (which is some 5 metres wide by 3 metres high) by using five sheets of corrugated iron stood on end, and held in place with an iron bar at chest height. The bar fits into a ring in the wall

---

[5]Star Trek reference

at one end, and is secured at the other end with a padlock. So the procedure to get the bike out is:

Unlock padlock.

Remove iron bar (which is rather heavy).

Remove one of the corrugated iron panels – being careful to avoid the electrical wire which runs across the upper part of the entrance – and prop it up against a wall.

Remove another one of the corrugated iron panels, and prop it up against the first.

For added clearance, remove another corrugated iron panel, and prop it up against the first two.

Then the motorcycle can be driven out. Ah, but we haven't finished!

Re-install first corrugated iron panel.

Re-install second corrugated iron panel.

Re-install third corrugated iron panel.

Replace iron bar.

Lock padlock.

Then, of course, once one has returned from one's trip, the whole procedure needs to be repeated. Except this time LSS's assistance is required to get the bike into the garage; because it needs to be wheeled in backwards. Of course this is not made any easier by the fact that the ground inside the building is not level, and the bike itself weighs nearly 300kg. Once the barn has been sorted out, we intend installing glass sliding doors. This will free up the current wooden doors so that they can be re-used for the garage. And hopefully by that point in time I will have laid a proper limecrete floor in the garage, perhaps with a small steel turntable so the bike can be spun around. But until all this has been done, going for a ride on the bike is not a simple event.

October

T HIS is the month for picking mushrooms! We also pick apples and chestnuts, and visit the Château de Chambord. Both our computers go pop. And we meet a real-life Obelix...

We have come to the conclusion that hens are funny creatures. When we arrive with their dinner bucket of soaked bread and kitchen scraps, they all cluster at the gate of the chicken coop, calling out:

"Pok. Pawkkk. Paaawwk. Paaaawrk. Pork! Pork! Pork! Porkporkporkporkpork!"

We've told them they're not getting any pork. Any pork in the vicinity gets eaten by us. So there.

As the weather has been suitable (damp and not too cold) I was invited mushroom-picking with T&M. His house, like ours, is surrounded by woodland. Except, unlike ours, it's not his woodland. So he gave strict instructions not to leave any footprints in any patches of mud we came across, and to walk quietly. I'd never been mushroom-poaching before.

Well, we ended up with a couple of baskets full of cep (*Boletus edulis*).

Near a rotting log, I also found some Amethyst Deceiver (*Laccaria amethystinea*), so gathered those. T was rather dubious about these as he had never seen them before, and didn't know that they were edible. His favourite is the girolle or chanterelle (*Cantharellus cibarius*). In his opinion there is no better mushroom. Personally I don't find that they have much taste.

We visited the Château de Chambord. It's that time of year when the red deer are in rut, and there are a lot of them in the castle grounds. This woodland comprises an area of some 5,260 hectares. They have constructed a sort of raised hide from which one can watch the deer. T&M wanted to see the spectacle, so we all went together, with T driving.

The Château was built by Francis I in the early sixteenth century as a hunting lodge. Although it is considered that he built it, I very much doubt that he personally wielded a bricklaying trowel. In fact history reports that he only spent a total of seven weeks there during his lifetime. At that time, there was no nearby village or estate, so the only available food was game. Therefore most of the food had to be brought in.

We spent a good few hours observing the deer; then as it was starting to get dark we visited the castle itself. Obviously we didn't go in, because it was closed at that time of day. But we strolled around the floodlit exterior, and took several photos of the castle with its reflection glimmering on the surface of the decorative moat. The number of chimneys on the roof was quite impressive.

On the way home T drove a lot more slowly, with good reason. Next to the road we suddenly saw a group of wild boar. You don't see them very well at night even with full headlights switched on, because they are dusty grey in colour, and their eyes do not reflect light, unlike deer or rabbits. Several large specimens crossed right in front of the car, completely unperturbed by our presence. A lot of people around here have had car accidents through unexpectedly hitting a boar or deer.

T&M invited us to go and visit T's grandmother. With an ulterior motive; we'd previously asked him if there was anywhere we could get a lot of apples, because our apple trees have produced almost nothing this year, and, as mentioned previously, we wanted to make some cider. Although our apple trees had a lot of blossom in spring, this was rapidly followed by a late frost, with the resultant lack of fruit. T's grandmother is aged 93, and she has an orchard. She already had as many apples as she could store, so as a reward for visiting her, told us to help ourselves to whatever we wanted. We came back with some 50kg of apples in bags. So the cider-making process can get under way! In the interim, we have 2 litres of wine in production. This is real wine, made from grapes. The grapevine next to the garage was the only vine which produced any grapes this year. There weren't that many, but they're not very nice to eat so we decided to try making wine with them. Yes, I know, 2 litres isn't much. It will only be a couple of bottles in the end – and we don't know if it will be any good! Still, if it isn't, we'll use it for cooking. I drew the line at stomping the grapes with my feet though. The current batch of beer fermenting quietly in a corner of the kitchen was made from real malted barley and hops this time, instead of a kit. The advantage of doing full-grain brewing here is that the hens love the mashed barley once the brewing is complete!

In a similar vein, it was LSS's birthday this month, so I made her some cookies. We have a hazel tree in the garden, and the hazelnuts are lovely, so I have several jars full – already shelled. I had decided to try making some hazelnut liqueur with some of them. At the end of the process I had a bowlful of alcohol-steeped chopped hazelnuts, so decided that these would be ideal ingredients for cookies. They were a hit. So now LSS wants me to make more hazelnut liqueur just so she can have more cookies! Of course they're made with our own free-range eggs. Oh, and the liqueur is rather tasty too. Mind you, one should only drink a thimbleful at a time as it's rather strong!

Visitors who have tasted our home-made produce - for example, the country wines - have asked us why we don't sell it. To which the reply is invariably "We're in the wrong country!"'

It would involve dealing with a tremendous amount of red tape and several governmental tax laws. So instead, we've entered the bartering system. For instance, we gave one of LSS's friends in the village some of our eggs and chestnuts, and in return we got a basket of apples and some tomatoes, as all our tomatoes failed this year. The system is working rather well.

The chestnut trees across from the house have once again produced a massive crop; the chestnuts are the size of golf balls. I've been shelling them and drying them, chopping them up and grinding them, and finally putting them in the food processor in order to make flour. As I make my own bread, I add 100g of chestnut flour to 300g of normal flour, and it makes the bread exceptionally tasty.

It's also been a very good year for mushrooms. So far we've eaten chanterelles, parasols and cep, and were also given a big bagful of hedgehog mushrooms (*Hydnum repandum*) by the local woodcutter, who has known LSS since she was little.

The reedbed is now practically finished; we need to get one more trailer-load of fine gravel, and then we can start planting the reeds. I have about another 10 metres of piping to connect up and entrench, and then the house greywater can go straight into the reedbed. No more emptying buckets! We've actually moved 12 tonnes of gravel by hand with shovel and wheelbarrow. It has taken a month and a half – although obviously we were not working on this exclusively.

LSS now has several more private students in addition to her contract work two days a week. In her spare time she has started painting the lounge. Because the walls are covered with plaster of paris which is a) not exactly smooth, b) very soft and c) comes off on your hand as a white powder, we've opted for an acrylic sandy-textured paint. In bright orange. But before you exclaim in horror, it's not as garish as it sounds. It does lend a feeling of warmth to the room – and with the boiler stove going it really looks cosy.

The farm next door was turned into a gîte (self-catering accomodation) a couple of years ago. They have now joined the 21st century and have a website; although not their own domain. Nevertheless, the website did need to be translated into English. So that was another little job for LSS. My assistance was required on the technical front regarding the actual HTML coding. In return, we asked them for a link to our own website. Another example of the bartering system in action!

As I mentioned previously, we have been looking forward to having our computers back in operation for a while now. Well, with the lounge finally ready and computer desks installed, I retrieved them from their cardboard boxes. Unfortunately the year-and-a-half of inaction had not been kind; neither would switch on. Some troubleshooting revealed that the power supplies have both died, so I have had to order some new ones. Aside from repairing this modern technology, the next project will be the installation of a central heating system run from the thermal store. This involves installing a radiator in the bedroom linked to a 12V pump, which will be controlled by a timer and thermostat.

Returning to the topic of home-brewing, cider-making is one of the enjoyable little tasks to be carried out at this time of year. That is to say, it's usually enjoyable. This year, however, we had no end of trouble. The first problem was the dearth of apples on the property. Fortunately, this was resolved by visiting T's grandmother.

Now, the simplified procedure for making cider is to break the apples into little pieces, press the little pieces to collect the juice, and then ferment the juice.

Some years ago, I constructed a machine for breaking apples into little pieces. Called a scratter, it is basically a rotating drum with lots of stainless steel screws protruding from its surface. This drum is located below a hopper, and it is powered by an old electric motor via a car fan belt.

No, this was not the second problem. The scratter did its job wonderfully, producing a large quantity of ground-up apples. I placed the apple mush into some lace-curtain-type material using a wooden form. The resultant parcel is known as a "cheese". Three cheeses were stacked on top of each other; a wooden board was placed on top, and the hydraulic jack was deployed. THIS was the next problem. Although this procedure had worked relatively well in the past, this time it didn't. For some reason the cheeses refused to stay put and be squeezed. They simply slid away from each other, pushing bits of apple everywhere. After several attempts, I was getting nowhere, becoming seriously annoyed, and was considering throwing the whole lot in the dustbin. Including the press.

At that particular moment, T&M chose to arrive. Being in a bad mood, I regret I was somewhat unwelcoming – especially when T typically started dispensing advice on the best way to press apples. Undaunted by my monosyllabic responses, he started telling me about this friend of his, who would be able to construct a new, improved version of my cider press at the drop of a hat. So, as I had nothing to lose, and was actually wearing a hat at the time, I got into T's car, and we went to visit this friend.

Now for reasons which will later become apparent, I'm going to be purposefully vague about names and places.

We turned into a property on the outskirts of a town, and stopped in front of an apparently-abandoned building with boarded-up windows, and what appeared to be a scrap-yard behind this dilapidated construction. T knocked on the weather-beaten front door, and one of the boarded-up windows opened a crack. An eye regarded us suspiciously through the gap. The window shut; the front door opened, and the friend appeared. I shall call him Mr. C.

T introduced us. After the usual pleasantries, T explained the problem.

"Seems like you need some sort of metal cylinder. Hmm. Let's have a look around and see what we've got," said Mr. C.

Glancing around furtively, he carefully shut the front door, and led the way into the scrapyard. We started looking.

After several minutes we found a length of large steel pipe. Unfortunately though, it was my opinion that the diameter was not quite large enough.

"Ah, wait a minute!" exclaimed Mr. C. "I have just the thing!"

Next to another pile of assorted scrap was a small 13kg butane gas cylinder. He grabbed the item and triumphantly carried it back to his workshop. I trotted along behind, assuming he was going to carry out some form of gas-torch-welding with it. How wrong I was...

Plonking it down on the concrete surface in front of his workshop, he rocked it from side to side.

"Oh. Not quite empty. Hang on a minute."

He disappeared into the workshop, and emerged with a large stilson wrench with which he started to unscrew the tap from the top of the cylinder. I retreated behind T's car, as did T. You see, Mr. C has a penchant for small cigars. There's always one dangling from the corner of his mouth. Lit, of course.

The tap came off. Mr. C grabbed the cylinder and inverted it, a pool of liquid butane forming around his feet. "Puff-puff" went the cigar.

"Good, it's empty. Now we can start."

Laying the cylinder on its side, he grabbed a convenient angle grinder, planted a large boot on the cylinder, and started cutting; all the while puffing away on the cigar. There was a tremendous "WHUFFF!" as the remaining gas in the cylinder ignited from the angle grinder sparks.

Mr. C did not turn a hair – or lift his boot. *" 'pas grave!"* ("Not serious!") he called out, lifting his head to see where we were. All he could have seen would have been the top portion of our heads as we peered over the bonnet of T's car, behind which we were cowering.

With the top of the cylinder removed, he then clamped the bottom half into his large metalworking lathe and smoothed off the rim. The top part was treated similarly, and a metal brace was welded in place. His idea was that the top would be inverted, and could be pushed down inside the cylinder, squeezing the apples and extracting the juice. It was then my job to drill lots of holes in the bottom of the cylinder to allow the juice to flow out.

So, did it work? Like a charm. Although I later modified the press slightly. The rounded shape of the top was not ideal; I replaced it with a thick disc made from an off-cut of melamine-faced kitchen counter top. I also drilled more holes in the sides to enable the juice to flow out more quickly. Now, instead of a lace curtain, an old pillowcase holds the crushed apples, and once pressing has been carried out, what remains (called pomace) is practically dry.

We now have just over 20 litres of apple juice quietly fermenting. Neighbour T became fascinated with the whole home-brewing concept, so purchased a beer kit, consisting of a tin of malt extract with a packet of yeast. He has borrowed one of my fermentation bins. I think the home-brewing community has another convert!

And what about Mr. C? Well, as recompense for his assistance, we later took him two bottles of cider.

We have since discovered more interesting things about Mr. C. He's considerably shorter than I, and could best be described as "stocky". He has a very generous nature, and after every visit we've come away clutching jars containing such delicacies as wild boar pâté, or home-made sausages. The latter are made in 20-metre lengths (yes really) using a home-built hydraulic sausage-stuffing machine. A home-made vacuum sealer is then used to make handy packages for the freezer. He recently rescued twenty battery hens, and now uses the resulting eggs to make his own pasta.

He's self-employed and does house clearances for a living, but on a larger scale. In other words, a landlord will call him up if there is a factory or office building which needs to be emptied of all its equipment, often prior to demolition taking place. His services are quite in demand because he has a reputation for getting the job done quickly. This is not surprising as he is one of those rare persons who do not need much sleep. When he was younger, he would start work on Monday morning, and finish on Friday evening – not stopping for anything as mundane as sleep. He would then sleep from Friday evening until Monday. In other words, he would have worked without sleep for 120 hours. No, I didn't think it was possible either. He chuckles when recounting this. "Of course

I can't do that any more. Nowadays I need at least two hours sleep per night."

He also only eats one meal a day, at lunchtime. What is lacking in frequency is made up by quantity. The meal is usually something like pasta – at least 1kg uncooked weight – with whatever accompaniments are on the menu that day. Now you can understand why we consider him to be a modern-day Obelix.

One other characteristic he shares with the cartoon character who-fell-into-the-magic-potion-when-he-was-a-baby, is tremendous strength. The following example was related to us by someone else (and was later confirmed by Mr. C himself):

Mr. C happened to be undertaking some building clearance work in Paris. One of the approach roads to the site had a very narrow section, only allowing the passage of one vehicle at a time. A sign at the approach to this obstacle indicates which vehicle has priority; if other vehicles are engaged one has to simply wait until the road is clear. Next to the waiting areas, the authorities have installed low concrete bollards, for reasons known only to themselves. This is important, as will become apparent shortly.

Now Mr. C was second in line to go through the aforementioned narrow section. Once the oncoming traffic had crossed, he noticed that the vehicle in front was not moving, so he carried out the typical French manoeuvre of leaning on the horn button. There were several other vehicles behind him at this point, and they joined in the chorus. The driver of the vehicle in front was using his mobile phone, and showed a rather rude sign through the window with his free hand.

This was like a red rag to a bull for Mr. C. He got out of his van, and walked around to the front of the offending vehicle, where he bent down in front of it and took hold of the bumper. He then straightened his legs and walked several paces to the left before carefully lowering the front of the vehicle onto the concrete bollards. An unexpected silence fell on the scene, as all the hooting from the vehicles behind suddenly stopped. Now that the path to the narrow section was clear of obstruction, Mr. C returned to his van and calmly continued his journey, leaving the hapless offender to figure out how to extricate himself from his predicament.

He has his own code of conduct; not paying much regard to the official laws. Prior to moving to his current location, he had rented a workshop in a nearby town. The roof started leaking badly, so he informed the landlord. Nothing was done, so he simply told the landlord he would cease paying rent until the roof was fixed.

Of course the landlord did not take kindly to this, and stated that he would report the matter to the police if the outstanding rent was not paid.

The rent was not paid. The police were called. The case went to court, and Mr. C was sentenced to six months in gaol. He chuckled at that as well. "It didn't do him any good, of course. That idiot of a landlord still didn't get his money!"

November

H OME-brewing is started in earnest by T&M. The reedbed is complete, and I design and install a central heating system. The electricity upgrading continues, and EDF cuts some tree branches with a scary-looking trimming machine.

The reedbed is finally operational. In the end it took three trailer loads of fine gravel (totalling over 1500kg) to spread on top of the coarser gravel.

In the interim we looked at the prices of reeds (*Phragmites australis*) from garden centres and online, but at a price of €4 per plant (minimum!), we opted for plan B. LSS collected some wild reeds instead, carefully digging them up from some roadside ditches on her way to various locations to give English lessons. These have now been planted in the gravel, and the greywater piping has been connected up.

The reed planting is a bit of an experiment because we're heading into the winter. I have some other reeds installed in plant-pots submerged in the pond, ready for installation in the reedbed in spring. If the current reeds in the reedbed don't survive the winter, we'll just replace them. It's difficult to identify the type of reed at this stage; I doubt they're *Phragmites* – in fact some may be *Typha* (bulrushes) – but I don't think it should matter too much. After all, the purpose of the plant is to take oxygen down to the roots where it can be made available to the bacteria which do the actual cleaning of the water. We'll see how they do. It's only grey water that they have to clean, so there is no concern about pathogens.

In fact we're also using ecological dishwasher detergent. No chlorine bleach allowed!

There has been complete silence from the Mairie regarding our solar thermal panel on the roof. So this means we can go ahead with the installation. Which means I need to start constructing it!

LSS came into the house the other day to inform me that we had a new hen, and to bring the camera. Puzzled, I followed her to the chicken coop. Unfortunately, because I'd brought the camera, the subject of the intended photograph had moved. Which, as any photographer knows, is usually the case.

The new hen in question had been curled up comfortably in one of the nests, and had been studiously ignored by the other hens. As we entered the chicken coop, it stretched, yawned, and jumped down to come and greet us, purring.

Yes, it was our cat. She wasn't interested in the hens, so we can only assume she's done this before. She had probably asked herself the usual question: "Ooh, it moves. Can I eat it?" followed by second thoughts: "Hmm, no... it's too big. And there are four of them. I'll ignore them instead."

I've now installed a new central heating radiator in the bedroom; I still need to connect up the piping to the thermal store and construct a control panel which will house the timer, thermostat and temperature gauges (all of which run on 12 volts DC – planning ahead for when we install a photovoltaic solar panel.) The control panel will contain a simple electrical logic circuit which I've designed so that if the temperature in the thermal store goes over 70° C, the 12V pump will switch on, thus using the bedroom radiator as a heat dump. The pump will also switch on at certain times of day. More on the construction of this later.

A start has also been made on the upgrading of the electric circuit in the bedroom. I've removed all the old wiring, and at the moment we are running a temporary extension lead from the lounge. Mind you, all it needs to power are the bedside lights, clock, and cordless telephone.

I mentioned previously that the computer power supplies had both died. Well, the replacements arrived within a week. I started with LSS's pc, and installed the new power supply. When I switched it on, the motherboard promptly went "phut".

So, I ordered a new motherboard. And because technology has moved on, this meant a new processor as well.

And new memory modules.

When all these bits had arrived the computer now had a 2.6GHz dual-core processor with 4Gb RAM. I installed the operating system.

Then the hard disk died... Aaargh!

Fortunately, having worked in IT, I had a couple of spare hard disks, but this meant I had to install everything again. I do keep disk images on backup, but as the operating system was also being changed, these were of no use. Once everything was installed, I did another disk image – if LSS's hard disk fails again it will be a simple 15-minute job to change the disk and re-image it.

Once LSS's computer was up and running, I turned my

attention to my own pc, and installed the new power supply. I then discovered that, like the other one, this one's motherboard had also gone pop. So, once again, I've ordered a new motherboard, processor and RAM. I selected the same specifications as LSS's computer in order to simplify driver installation. I'm sure once they arrive I'll discover that my hard disk has died too. But this should not be such an issue – as I'm not changing my own operating system I'll be able to use my backup disk image. At least now there is no competition for the laptop...

I'm afraid our neighbour T has definitely caught the home-brewing bug in earnest. He was so impressed with the results from his first malt-extract beer kit that he has bought some fermentation vessels and sundry other bits; and is now looking for a 200-litre stainless steel tank in order to start making beer on a larger scale – which he then intends selling. Well, he may as well try! He's been unemployed for 5 years so this may be a business opportunity for him. He has been hinting rather heavily that I should join him in this venture; but I'm not that keen. I have enough to do around here as it is, and I brew beer just for the pleasure of it, not to make money out of it. Besides, this would then involve all sorts of governmental red tape, liquor licences, and various other regulations. No thanks.

A week or so later, T was pleased to give me an update on his brewing venture. He was given two stainless steel 30-litre beer kegs by a friend. Apparently they had been gathering dust in a garage for years. The thing is: they were both still full! T managed to get the bung out of the first one, but the beer it contained was completely flat. It was obviously a mass-produced beer, and had probably started life as something like Kronenbourg 1664. I suspect the gas to make it bubbly would probably have been added as it went through a beer dispenser, but not being an expert on mass-produced beer I decided to experiment. I recovered about 20 litres of it, and added some malt extract, sugar, and beer yeast. We'll see if that adds some bubbles back into it!

T then emptied the other keg down the drain, and took both of them around to Mr. C so he could cut the tops off on his metalworking lathe – thus converting them into a mash tun and wort boiler. Apparently micro-breweries are becoming all the rage in the UK at the moment, so his idea of brewing and selling beer looks quite feasible.

We visited the Christmas Market in Brinon with T&M. We didn't buy anything, though; it was mainly food and handmade trinkets. Afterwards we were invited back to T&M's place to taste his latest beer. This was also made from a beer kit and was quite good. My only complaint was that he has elected to use the ubiquitous 330ml bottles. Well, he was given a lot of empties by his brother, so I suppose it's logical. Personally, I use proper beer bottles for my brews: English pints. He has been researching the brewing process, and has decided he wants to create his own recipes using malted barley and hops. LSS told me that she has the impression that his brewing business won't get very far, because he'll get too involved in trying to create the perfect recipe instead of just making a good beer and then selling it. I guess time will tell.[6]

The following week, T requested my assistance in loading and unloading his van. He had found a malt house which sells to the public in a town called Issoudun. Their minimum quantity order is a 25kg bag, so I'm sure he would have been able to load and unload on his own. But I went along for the ride anyway. He ended up buying four bags, with three different types of malt. Now he's ready to start brewing his own recipes. On the way back we passed through a town called Reuilly which is well-known for its wine, so he stopped for a quick tasting, and ended up buying a few bottles.

Unfortunately, the kegged beer he gave me and which I attempted to re-ferment did absolutely nothing. They had obviously added some sort of preservatives to it. Regretfully I poured it onto the compost heap, as it didn't taste very nice at all.

EDF (France Electricity) were in the vicinity recently. They came past the property with their tractor in order to clear tree branches from the proximity of the pylon-mounted electricity mains cable. We're the last house on the grid. The machinery they were using reminded me of that James Bond film – it was a hydraulically-operated arm at the end of which were several large vicious-looking circular saw blades. After they'd gone I went along the road and collected all the larger branches which I brought back to cut up for firewood. Well, there's no point in wasting it, is there?

---

[6]Spoiler alert: LSS was right.

Unfortunately our plan of making sloe wine this year has hit a bit of a snag. You see, you're supposed to wait until you get the first frost before picking the sloes. This tenderises them. Well, we left it a bit too late and there aren't any sloes left on the trees - the birds and the wind have conspired to remove them all! Oh well, there's always next year. There are still twelve days to go before the next batch of beer is ready to drink; which is a good thing as we're now down to the last bottle of the previous batch of bitter!

This month the cat took her annual trip to the vet for her vaccination booster injection. Apparently this is somewhat of a rarity around here; it seems cat owners do not usually bother with this little chore. So the vet was extremely happy to see us. Cat, of course, was not extremely happy to see the vet. She didn't seem to mind the car journey though, unlike our previous feline.

It has also turned frosty in the mornings. I wouldn't be surprised if we had snow soon. We have the kitchen range going from dawn to dusk now, and we also light the boiler stove at around 4 p.m. so we can have a hot bath in the evening. It's a good job we have a lot of wood stacked up! I must admit I've tended to avoid doing any work outside recently.

I'm pleased to report the bedroom radiator circuit is working as designed.

One of our hens has become confused, thinking that day is night and night is day. So she's now laying an egg from her night-time perch every night. Wheeeeeeeee......splat. We thought it was an isolated incident at first, but after she'd done it twice in a row, I put some extra straw under their perches. Now it's wheeeeeeeeeee...... (soft bounce). It's been going on for a week. Silly bird.

December

I SWEEP the kitchen chimney. More wood joins the wood-shed, and Neighbour J comes to Christmas lunch where she has her first taste of a Rumtopf.

It has now turned cold in earnest. And although we don't watch television, we do keep up to date with the news. There have been major problems in coastal areas due to heavy rain. However because we're so far inland we have not had any flooding here; in fact we haven't had any rain for a couple of weeks now.

It was minus 7 degrees C last night so the pond has frozen over. Despite the cold it's actually fairly pleasant having a bath in the evenings. We carry the bathtub into the kitchen from its customary place in the front garden, and put it on a couple of wooden planks next to the wood stove, where it's toasty warm. The planks keep the drain connection off the floor; otherwise the bath wouldn't be very stable! We then add hot water via the flexible pipe and garden tap which I had installed under the kitchen sink, for just this purpose. We tend not to fill the bath too much, because afterwards we have to carry it out into the front garden again. The following morning it gets emptied with a bucket, and this waters the garden at the same time. Of course, as it's now winter, one has to break the ice first before it can be emptied.

I recovered yet another fallen tree, the wood of which will go into the woodshed ready for the winter in two years' time. Yes, we already have sufficient for this year and the next! The shifting of heavy logs does tend to make my back ache a bit though.

Even though I had cut the trunk into 30cm sections, each section must measure some 2 metres in circumference – I estimate each one weighs around 80kg. So I was heaving the pieces into the transport box on the rear of the tractor – only 3 would fit at a time – and then driving them back home where I offloaded. It took me three trips. Now the fun starts, splitting them into firewood-shaped bits with a splitting maul! I'm not complaining, mind you; I enjoy the physical work.

Speaking of trees, as they are now dormant, I made a start at clearing the brush and brambles around three of our apple trees, and pruning off dead and unwanted branches. There are another four trees which I still need to tackle. I cut some of the branches into short lengths and have stored them in old wooden fruit-boxes in the workshop. I plan to use the wood to create apple-smoked meat at a later date. I've also kept a box full of oak shavings for the same reason. And considering the shavings, there is one article of farm equipment which would come in very handy; perhaps we'll keep an eye on the sales. It's a branch chipper and shredder. A petrol-powered one would be ideal; although I have access to a tractor I don't really want to go the whole hog by getting a PTO-powered wood chipper at this stage. Besides, they are a LOT more expensive.

On the language front, I suspect you were wondering how my French is coming along; seeing as this is our second year here. Well, it's improving, but as I am doing all the household renovations and construction myself, I don't have the opportunity to practice much. And as the television is only used for watching DVD's, I don't watch French programmes. The only persons I see fairly regularly are M&O, and T&M. T tends to want to practice his English rather than me practising my French. Now I wouldn't exactly say I had a flair for languages. Although I learned Afrikaans at school I was not exactly fluent. Until, that is, I trotted off to University. Stellenbosch was the only university in Africa which offered a degree in my chosen field, forestry. Lo and behold, all the lectures were in Afrikaans. I struggled badly for the first couple of months and then suddenly something "clicked". I found I was listening to the lecture in Afrikaans and writing notes in English without having to think about it. So I've been hoping something similar will happen with French. I understand it fairly well and I'm starting to put sentences together.

It's complicated though. Unlike English or Afrikaans, all French nouns have sexes. Actually so do German nouns; but my German is now practically non-existent as I haven't spoken it since 1979! However, unlike German, where each noun has a capital letter and the sex of the noun just changes the "the" e.g. *der Tisch* : the table – masculine; or *das Auto* : the car – neutral; or *die Dame* : the lady – feminine, in French the sex of the noun in the sentence also determines the form of any adjective. Which is all very confusing.

For example, "I bought a new hat" is:

"j'ai acheté un nouveau chapeau" - (hat being, of course, male. Well, it's obvious, isn't it? Er... no.)

Not *"j'ai acheté une nouvelle chapeau"*.

So I tend to make quite a few mistakes like that. And they switch things around too. For example, a catfish is not, as you may think, *un chat poisson*. But instead *un poisson chat* – a fish cat. Which, by the way, is male. Even when it's female.

And take the phrase, "next year". I keep saying *"prochaine anné"* instead of *"anné prochaine"*. My head hurts.

Oh well. I can at least read it and make sense of what I'm reading. And people understand what I'm trying to say. They keep saying to LSS "But you must teach him French"! The thing is, LSS and I speak English to each other – we have done so for 15 years so that isn't about to change! Mind you, this language malarkey can come in handy on the odd occasion I answer the telephone. When I diagnose it's a cold caller trying to sell us something, I normally purposefully mangle the French, saying in essence "I don't speak French, do you speak English?"

To which the reply is usually "Oh! No I don't, terribly sorry, goodbye." Although there was one occasion when a chap replied (in English) "Actually, yes, I do. We are trying to, um, er, erm..." (click).

I think he suddenly realised his English wasn't quite as good as he thought.

The hens are still laying 3 eggs per day on average. It will be interesting to see their reaction when it snows! "Paaawwwk! What's this white stuff? Can I eat it?" Probably due to the shortage of available food elsewhere, lots of little birds have started visiting the garden. We see various finches, wrens, the usual robins – and there is usually a woodpecker tapping away in the background somewhere. It's a twitcher's paradise here!

On the beer front, I brewed some Victoria Bitter. It should be ready to drink early next year. Although I have made beer from malted barley before (this is called all-grain brewing) I much prefer using the kits. It's quicker and certainly easier. These generally consist of a large tin of malt extract, which has already been boiled with hops, and most of the water removed. All one needs to do is add sugar, water and yeast. And if one uses the kit as a basis, it can always be improved by the addition of ingredients like spraymalt or ground coriander. It's much cheaper (and nicer) than buying factory-produced beer. I think our Christmas tipple this year will be home-made cider. We have sampled it. It tastes very nice although it's not quite as effervescent as I had hoped it would be.

Christmas is approaching rapidly. We've decided we're not going to do much. We're just going to put our feet up and catch up on watching some DVD's. The Christmas tree has now been retrieved from a box in the barn and dusted off, and LSS spent an enjoyable afternoon decorating it.

We've already been stuffing our faces with chocolates. Only in the evenings though, so I don't think anyone will notice. From the look of the online weather forecasts it doesn't look like we'll be having a white Christmas after all.

I can't believe how quickly this year has gone. As usual, we're not having turkey. There's no point in cooking a great big bird when there's only the two of us. Instead a leg of wild boar is already marinating in a large dish. The marinade base is home-made sloe wine! It should be interesting...

Oh yes - and we've also tested the Rumtopf, which we started in June. Oh my goodness. It smells wonderful, but I'm not too sure if we'll do it again. The plums: taste like rum. Strawberries: taste like rum. Blackberries: taste like rum. Pears... well, you get the idea. I think it needs to be served with ice cream. As a sauce. In a small glass. Not a soup-bowl full like we had last night. It's a good job we both like rum.

We've invited Neighbour J to come and have lunch with us on Christmas Day. This is the lady with the impressive moustache. If she does agree to join us for lunch, it will be a miracle; as she really doesn't like leaving her farm for anything. Her shopping is done for her by M&O; and as for clothing, she uses catalogues and places telephone orders. She's lived there all her life, and never married.

Unfortunately once her parents died her brother took over the running of the farm, and did not allow her to have any boyfriends either. Now that he's passed away as well, she's quite happy on her own. In her late 60's, she's still very active although she's bent double – probably from carrying heavy milk churns around. As for the livestock, she still has four elderly cows. Chickens roam freely around the farmyard and are regularly decimated by foxes. There are dozens of rabbit cages, with furry occupants. And there are cats. Oh my goodness are there cats. Although she cares for them, none of them have ever been near a vet. So they're covered in fleas.

And have worms. And none of them are spayed or neutered, so there are several litters of kittens every year.

Her weekly shopping list includes a large bag of dry dog food. For the cats. Why dog food? Who knows? Maybe it's cheaper. She says they like it. Well, if it's the only food there is, of course they'd like it. Mind you, there aren't any mice around. And although one should not give cows' milk to cats, as Neighbour J has cows, guess what the cats get? Correct. But the thing is, if cats don't like living somewhere, they simply leave. So it would seem they're fairly happy there.

Her farmhouse is an absolute mess. The large kitchen table is simply buried underneath piles and piles of newspapers and other rubbish; there's a small space along one edge just large enough for her to fit a plate, or for any guests to put their coffee cups. The only source of heating is the kitchen range, which was probably installed soon after the house was built. It smokes a bit. And, as is common around here, there is no evidence of an indoor bathroom. We suspect that one of the outbuildings possibly contains some sort of toilet, but we've been afraid to ask. As an eccentric, she's near the top of the list. But she has a heart of gold.

A week or so ago we were given some packets of leaf tea by one of LSS's friends, so we're having proper tea for once. I normally just drink coffee. Mind you, we unforunately no longer have a teapot. LSS has ordered one online but it hasn't arrived yet – so we're having to resort to brewing the tea in a Pyrex measuring jug.

The week before Christmas, the weather turned blustery and squally, but I'm pleased to report our earthenware-tile-covered roof is withstanding all the water which is falling upon it. The gutters are doing a sterling job, and all the excess water is gushing out into the pond, which is filling up nicely.

On Christmas Eve we sat peacefully with the boiler stove crackling away, each of us quaffing a pint of home-brewed Belgian Ale. The nibbles toasted nicely in the kitchen range, and I activated an automated music DJ selecting songs at random from my collection of MP3 files. By the way, if you have a large collection of music I can recommend the program MusicBee (free download). LSS has given the carers the day off tomorrow, so will be looking after the Aged FIL herself.

Christmas Day dawned. Much to our surprise, Neighbour J did indeed come for lunch! LSS fetched her after having tended to the Aged FIL in the morning. She seemed to enjoy herself, and quite liked the roast wild boar. Mind you, her eyes went a bit squiffy after having had some rumtopf dessert. We poured her into the car and LSS took her back home.

We didn't do very much on Boxing Day, but the following day we encountered a small problem. The kitchen range had started to smoke and was not drawing very well, so I suspected I knew what the problem was. I was right. The 6" diameter stovepipe was somewhat clogged with soot, leaving only about a 2" gap for the smoke to escape.

I have a vacuum cleaner for my workshop, so used that in addition to the usual chimney brush. However, at one point the vacuum cleaner hose became blocked with chunks of soot, so I put it to my mouth and blew down it. That resolved the problem, but had an unforeseen effect on LSS when she saw me. She doubled over with laughter. It was only when I looked in a mirror that I saw what was so funny. Do not blow down a vacuum cleaner's hose after having used it on soot; it leaves a black ring around your mouth. Still, at least the kitchen range is no longer smoking.

On the last day of the year, we didn't see the New Year in. We nearly made it; having watched some films on the laptop, but actually went to bed before midnight.

January

R EPAIRS to the thermal store take place. The Renault
5 has issues. I tan a coypu skin, and try my hand at
blacksmithing.

Actually, I suppose it's about time I told you something
about our village, Pierrefitte-sur-Sauldre.

The name Pierrefitte is derived from the Latin, *ficta petra*.
This means "stuck stone" and probably referred to a menhir
which was erected to mark the field boundary between two
Gaulish tribes; the Carnutes to the north and the Bituriges to
the south. The village later became a key point on the Roman
road between Orleans and Bourges until a faster route was
constructed, bypassing Pierrefitte completely. The Sauldre is
a river passing through the village. It flows north-west from
its source near the village of Montigny, and empties into the
river Cher.

Speaking of Gaulish tribes, in the past there was some
considerable argument between the councils of Pierrefitte and
the neighbouring village of Souesmes (pronounced "swem")
regarding the construction and maintenance of the bridge over
the river Sauldre. You see, the bridge is right on the outskirts
of Pierrefitte. The boundary of Souesmes starts in the middle
of the bridge. And yet, if you look at a map, Souesmes is
several kilometres away.

So why does the Souesmes boundary start so close to
Pierrefitte, and not logically half-way between the two
villages?

Well, the tale begins in the 18th century; and it's all the fault of the Pierrefitte Priest.

You see, he was a short, fat and rather clumsy individual, with a fondness for good food and wine. At that time there was no bridge, just a ford. And there was also no consensus of opinion as to where exactly the boundary between the two villages was.

Now the priest of Souesmes on the other hand was a tall, athletic, younger fellow. One day he was having a chat with his Pierrefitte counterpart; and the conversation came around to the Souesmes/Pierrefitte boundary. They decided that together, they would once and for all resolve the issue of the location of the boundary. Their bright idea was that they would have a race. On a chosen day, at noon, each would start out from his own village church, and run towards the other. Where they met: that would be the boundary.

Well the date and time arrived, and the Pierrefitte priest started out. Unfortunately it had rained that week, so the river was somewhat higher than normal. He got half-way across the ford before becoming stuck in the mud. He was unable to extricate himself, so he was still there when the priest from Souesmes arrived. And where they met, became the boundary.

Because of this, arguments over which council was responsible for the maintenance of the bridge dragged on for years. I believe it has now been resolved; with neither being responsible. Instead it's the regional Department of Transport.

Pierrefitte has a "four flower" ranking. This probably doesn't mean much to you, so I'll explain. In 1959 a nationwide annual competition was launched with the goal of increasing the attractiveness of towns and villages to visitors. This beautifying of communities was carried out by the planting of flowers, and the provision and maintenance of green spaces. Judging of the efforts of the municipality is carried out once a year, and the town or village is then allowed to display a road sign at their entrances proclaiming the result. The awards range from one flower, to the highest possible score of four flowers. Now this is all very well. At first glance the village certainly is pretty. But unfortunately the effect is somewhat spoilt when you look more closely. The village itself is not exactly thriving. The only shops are:

- A bakery. The bread is passable. The *patisserie* (cakes and things) is good albeit expensive. However, the baker's wife – who is the person at the counter selling the goods – is a miserable so-and-so. I don't think anyone has seen her smile. This has the unfortunate result of seriously limiting the amount of time (and money) one wants to spend in there. This is in stark contrast to the bakery in the nearby town where we now prefer to buy our bread. The assistants there are always smiling and chatty.

- A general store. Obviously the items are a lot more expensive than the supermarket. Trade isn't exactly booming. In fact the owner has attempted suicide. Twice.

- A café/tobacconist/newsagent. It's not doing very well.

This owner also attempted suicide, but was more successful than the owner of the general store. His widow is trying to sell the place, but there are no takers.

- A restaurant. Open only by appointment; with a correspondingly high price tag on the menu.

- A hairdresser. This business is booming. Well, the elderly village ladies do like to have their hair done!

There is no longer a butcher's shop. It closed because the owner retired, and nobody was interested in taking over.

A large number of houses in the village have their shutters closed. This is either because nobody lives in them at all; or because the owners are Parisians who only spend a few weeks there every year. One house in particular falls into the first category. It belongs to somebody in another town, and has been up for sale for years. However the owner refuses to budge on the ridiculously-high asking price, so as a result it is falling into serious disrepair. The gates are rusty; one of the chimneys is collapsing; shutters are hanging off their hinges; and the porch is falling down. Perhaps aptly, it is number 13.

The other problem with the four-flower award is the large wooden boxes of flowers which were installed. These have been placed in the roadway running past the Mairie to act as chicanes, in between several speed humps – which themselves are of non-standard height and bear many scars caused by caravan tow bars. Unfortunately this is also the main road between Souesmes and Chaon. And this route is the only one available to logging trucks. The fact that these huge articulated vehicles manage to negotiate the chicanes at all is a testament to the skill of the drivers. Actually, we have since discovered that not all of the drivers are quite so skilled. But the Mairie has a stack of these boxes in reserve to replace those mangled by the occasional unskilled driver.

The other roads in the village may not have speed humps or chicanes. But because of the usual shortage of funds, this does not mean one can drive from A to B without due care and attention. The poorly-repaired potholes demand constant vigilance.

The village church is rather pretty. But even there, all is not as it seems. It was struck by lightning in 1937 and burnt down. It was of course rebuilt, but due to cost constraints, instead of the previously oak-framed and panelled vaulted chapel ceiling, they used concrete.

The village itself used to be surrounded by earthen ramparts and ditches. These are no longer present; but at one place a boundary wall replaced the rampart, and can still be seen. It is now part of the external wall of the cemetery. Just outside the village are several burial mounds, reputedly those of Gaulish warriors. If you didn't know what they were, you would certainly overlook them; they're not exactly spectacular.

The population census gives the current number of inhabitants (which strangely enough includes us!) as 832. The highest population ever recorded was the dizzying number of 1,601. However, this was back in the year 1906.

Malaria was endemic in this region due to the prevalence of marshy areas. Land management practices in the 19th century contributed to the drying out of the swamps, and the disease was eradicated by the start of the 20th century. We still get large amounts of mosquitoes in summer though.

With the New Year celebrations over, we paid a visit to T&M's grandmother. As she had given us lots of apples, it was only fair to take her a couple of bottles of cider. She was quite delighted, as she had certainly not expected it! We had the obligatory coffee, and she seemed quite interested in what we were doing with the farmhouse renovation. The discussion eventually worked its way around to rabbits; and she mentioned that her father used to tan the skins. She then searched through one of the drawers in the kitchen, and came up with a piece of paper containing the recipe for tanning, which I was allowed to copy for future reference.

I've ordered a new battery for LSS's Hyundai. At its last servicing in the UK the mechanic recommended a new one, offering to install it straight away. Fortunately LSS declined. It's still the original battery, but is now ten years old. Although it has not given any problems, it's probably just as well to replace it. Actually I do have an ulterior motive; it's time to play "musical batteries". You see, the battery of the Renault 5 has died. This is the "spare" vehicle which I can use if LSS is out somewhere and I need a car. It's also useful for transporting stuff around the property. So the Renault 5 will get the Hyundai's old battery. It's temporarily using the battery from the Aged FIL's Citroen, which is slightly too big for the battery compartment.

I have been researching tankless water heaters. Our hot water is being supplied via the thermal store, which is currently being heated by the boiler stove. This is fine for the winter, but in summer it may be a bit warm to have the boiler stove going. I've already made a start on the solar thermal panel construction by painting an uncut sheet of plywood which will form the base. But thinking about it, if we have cloudy days I fear this solar panel won't be able to heat the water sufficiently. I figured a tankless water heater would be ideal as a backup heat source. However, we don't particularly want to get an electric one. Which leaves the only option being a gas-powered water heater. And unfortunately they're all rather expensive. I've decided we'll do without. If we have to light the boiler stove during the summer, so be it.

The Renault 5 was obviously aware of its impending "new" battery, because the starter motor has just died. I've ordered a replacement. I would love to have something like a 4×4 Isuzu pick-up instead for running around the farm; the tractor is just too much of a lump – and I noticed yesterday that one of its front wheels has gone flat. Again. Oh joy.

So far this year the weather hasn't been too bad. In fact it's actually unseasonably warm, with temperatures around the 10 degree mark. I have known it to get down to minus 20.

We visited some garden centres to have a look at petrol-engined wood chippers. One of these would be ideal to:
a) get rid of all the small branches and twigs which we have piled up and
b) make lots of lovely mulch for the garden!
Unfortunately nothing was available in the shops we visited. It looks like I'll need to buy one online.

The thermal store sprang a leak. LSS suddenly noticed a discoloured patch on the lounge ceiling. Actually the ceiling discolouration is my fault; I did install a drip tray in which the thermal store sits, but I had insulated the cylinder right down to the floor level with glass fibre, with the result that "wicking" took place, channelling some of the water out of the drip tray and onto the floor. The drip tray itself was actually doing its job, conducting water to the outside via the installed hosepipe.

I half-drained the tank, and used some leak-fix putty on the problem area, which is where the hot water supply coil exits the tank. Once the putty had set, I filled the tank again. It seems to have cured the problem. However, I've learned my lesson; no more insulating water tanks with glass fibre! Instead I'm going to wrap it with bubble wrap, followed by a layer of aluminium foil, followed by another two layers of bubble wrap.

But it could have been worse; there was only a small puddle on the floor upstairs. The discoloured patch in the ceiling can be repainted when it's dried out.

We've now started letting the hens free-range in the afternoons, with the result that:

a) we don't need to feed them quite as much due to all the worms and grubs and other bits and pieces they scratch up, and

b) they seem to enjoy it so much that we're now getting 4 eggs a day. They go back to their nesting boxes to lay.

The coypu skin has also now been tanned. I may make it into a Russian-style fur hat. Oh yes, I haven't told you about that yet. Well, I'd previously mentioned to T&M that I was interested in tanning skins. Two days later T turned up with a coypu which a gamekeeper friend of his had killed. A coypu (or Nutria) is similar to a beaver except that it has a long round tail rather than flattened. They're a South American species which were first introduced to France in the early 1880's to be farmed for their fur. The meat is lean and low in cholesterol. The animals often escaped or were even purposefully released. Now, of course, they're seen as an invasive species which cause environmental damage.

So, I skinned it, and tanned the pelt using a solution of salt and sulphuric acid. LSS made a pâte from the meat. It did not have a very strong taste; a bit like hare. The tanning itself was a bit of an experiment; as we want to start keeping rabbits for food this year, I wanted to see whether home tanning was an option. I have my sights set on some rabbit-fur slippers! Also, we're going to ask Neighbour J to start keeping her rabbit skins for us – at the moment she just throws them onto the compost pile. And we dislike waste. I've seen that a rabbit-pelt bedspread can sell for over €2,000! Not surprising really as it's a lot of work. Anyway, the tanned coypu pelt turned out quite nicely, so it's definitely a viable procedure.

We were once again invited for another beer tasting at T&M. He's now brewed a few different types of beer: a brown, a blonde, and (my favourite) an ale to which he added orange peel and coriander during the boil phase. He's also managed to sell some bottles, albeit to his brother.

On the wood-splitting front, a minor disaster occurred. I've broken my Stanley lump hammer. The handle has come away from the lump bit. As I'm lacking a decent wood-splitting maul, I've been using the lump hammer with some steel wedges to split log pieces into firewood. Obviously it couldn't cope. However, I found a piece of thick-walled steel pipe in the scrap-metal pile, and took it around to T&M to see if I could use his forge to shape the end of the pipe so that it would fit into the hole in the head of the hammer. Well, I managed it. But it wasn't exactly perfect. Once I returned home I used my mig welder to try and fuse the two bits together, and thus ensure the head doesn't come off the handle again. I think it's time I got myself a decent splitting maul.

So, I suppose it's time I updated you on the bath-room progress. Well, we still don't have an actual bathroom. Yet we still manage to have a daily bath in the kitchen, by carrying the bathtub in and out again. Due to its location next to the kitchen range, one could even cook the dinner whilst in the bathtub. Of course frying things would be a bad idea as the hot oil could splatter on parts which do not like hot oil splattered on them.

But at least we can wash – and we have hot water on tap instead of having to heat buckets on the stove. There are quite a few of LSS's relatives who have houses in town with bathrooms, yet they only wash once a week. Then if you consider cases like Neighbour J (the one with the moustache), she does not have a bathroom at all. Her late brother was hospitalised for a while, and was exceedingly astonished when they told him that washing twice a month was not quite sufficient.

As for us, before we can have such a luxury as an indoor bathroom, we need to sort out the barn first. The dirt floor will need to be replaced by a proper solid floor; some walls will need to be constructed, a ceiling put in place, and of course all the plumbing installed. And, like everything here, it's all going to be done by a very small labour force indeed; viz. LSS and myself.

February

T HE hens lay their 541st egg. I start constructing a poly-tunnel, and purchase a wood-chipper. And a pair of blue tits decide they want to nest in the house.

Despite a lot of prevarication, I finally ordered a petrol-powered wood chipper online from Germany. I couldn't find one locally. I could have ordered the same model from a company in France but it would have been a lot more expensive. No, I don't understand it either. When it arrived, it was fairly easy to assemble. I've obviously tried it out, and am quite pleased with the results, although there are a couple of adjustments which need to be made to the machine itself. For example, the feed tube is covered with a rubber "safety flap" which tends to restrict the free passage of branches, especially if they have little twigs sticking out. I intend removing that, for a start. It's designed to prevent the machine operator from inserting their arm all the way into the feed tube and having their fingers chopped off. I think I have enough intelligence to know not to insert my arm full length into a wood chipper at full throttle. So we no longer have a large pile of branches, but a wooden barrel full of mulch. It's very useful for converting otherwise unused material into something useful. Or getting rid of bodies.

Ah, me and my bright ideas! I just create work for myself. The thing is, now that I have wood-chippered mulch available in large quantities, it would be silly not to put it to use. And what better use than for growing plants? However, with the uncertain weather we have had recently, the only way to ensure a good crop of – for example – tomatoes, is to have a greenhouse. Well, we do have some assorted panes of glass scavenged from the dark recesses of the Aged FIL's various outbuildings. But there are insufficient quantities for an entire greenhouse. Therefore, a polytunnel has joined the list of buildings to be constructed. The simplest method – apart from purchasing a ready-made one, which is contrary to our economical self-sufficiency philosophy – is to take lengths of plastic pipe, and form large hoops with them by fixing each end to the ground. These can then be covered with a sheet of clear plastic.

So I've made a start. The construction site selected is in line with the greywater reedbed, between the wood sheds and the garden. Several oak planks have been pressed into service to form the lower framework of the polytunnel. There are a lot of these stacked at the Aged FIL. They were originally used for concrete formwork, left over from when he had a business constructing lakes. For the plastic pipe, I cut some 6m lengths of 32mm diameter irrigation hose left over from the borehole installation. These form semicircles with a radius of 1.9m, so I should be able to stand upright inside. I hammered some iron bars into the ground at regular intervals, and the plastic pipe simply fits over these. The pipe was then fixed to the oak planks with long screws. Some clear plastic is required to form the actual polytunnel itself; we don't have anything remotely resembling that, so a visit to a garden centre was required.

This was duly done, and we returned with a large sheet of clear PVC. It's something like 7 metres wide and 12 metres long, so LSS and I had great fun attempting to manhandle it into place. Not. At least it wasn't a windy day, so in the end we managed it without too much loss of temper. I've re-used some other pieces of lumber from the Aged FIL to make a door-frame, and the only thing remaining is to construct a door with panels made from some of the off-cuts of the plastic sheeting.

In an effort to become more energy-efficient – and also to save ourselves some money on the electricity bill – last year I purchased some LED bulbs on Ebay, from a seller in China. Not that we have a huge electricity bill mind you; but as my mother used to say, "If you look after the pennies, the pounds will look after themselves." Anyway, the bulbs never arrived, and the seller asked me to wait a while longer. Of course when I finally lost patience, I discovered that the 45-day money-back Paypal guarantee had expired. I contacted Ebay, and fortunately they gave me a refund anyway. So I bought them from a different seller. The Aged FIL has an entire collection of light bulbs. The old incandescent type. The majority are of the 40-watt variety; his contribution to saving energy. Mind you, it's been a bit of a job sorting through them to see if they still work or not. Whenever a bulb stopped working, he would replace it, and then put the defunct bulb back with the others.

We've had rather a lot of rain this month. As I tend to keep up to date with events in the UK, we're not alone. There are flood alerts everywhere in Britain. We're not at any risk of flooding here though, as we're at a higher elevation.

Today the chickens laid their 541st egg. "So what?" I hear you cry. Well, egg number 540 was the financial break-even point. Through the sale of eggs to neighbours, they have now not only paid for themselves, but all their food too. Mind you, nowadays we let them out before lunch, and they ramble the countryside, laying waste to vast swathes of leaf litter in search of their next mouthful. They're really funny though. If you stand outside and call "Pork!" they come running! But now I have to keep my workshop door closed during the day, otherwise they're in there like a shot: "Oooh, what's in here? Anything to eat? How about under here? And on top of this? What's up there?" and they leave chicken poo everywhere.

Our neighbours T&M have become converts to home brewing. With Mr. C's assistance, T modified a couple of old stainless steel beer kegs, turning them into a mash tun and wort kettle, and not a month goes by without our being invited to a *dégustation*.

I must admit, although I sometimes do full-grain brewing, although using the BIAB (brew-in-a-bag) method, I prefer the liquid malt extract kits in a tin. It's much less work, and you can still modify the taste and strength of the final result as you desire. However, last year I ordered a couple of kits made by a company called Brewferm which I had mistakenly thought were the usual liquid malt-in-a-tin type. It turned out they weren't; instead being bags of malted barley grains. The problem is that our largest saucepan is only capable of holding

12 litres of liquid, so the first kit had to be cooked up in two batches. It was a bit of a procedure; for this particular recipe the malted barley needed to be heated to 50 degrees and kept at that temperature for 15 minutes, then at 62 degrees for 45 minutes, then at 70 degrees for 5 minutes. Then the liquid needed to be drained, and boiled with hops for an hour. Then it had to be cooled down before putting it in a fermenting bucket with yeast. Still, the end result is worth it – and it's a lot cheaper than shop-bought beer.

For the second kit, I borrowed T's mash tun, and brewed the full 20 litres of beer, although still using the BIAB method.

I also extracted the two demijohns of perry (pear cider) from the outbuilding where they had been stored since October last year. I racked them to remove the sediment, and have just finished bottling that.

Next on the list is the bottling of the blackberry wine. After that, the demijohns will be empty, so we intend filling them again by brewing another batch of parsnip wine as we still have some parsnips in the garden.

Speaking of parsnip wine, last night the first batch was ready to drink. The taste has even improved somewhat over the six-month storage period. I think we'll be repeating this brew. In fact, I'll even include the recipe here, just in case you want to make some yourself:

Parsnip Wine Recipe:
Ingredients (makes 1 gallon or 4.5 litres):

- 1.8kg parsnips

- 1kg sugar

- 1 orange

- 1 lemon - (or instead of the orange and lemon, just use 1.5 tsp citric acid – this works just as well)

- 1 level tsp pectic enzyme (pectolase)

- 1 level tsp nutrient salts (for the yeast)

- 1 Vitamin B1 tablet (also for the yeast)

- Wine yeast

Method:

Wash and peel the parsnips. Note: peeling is not necessary for making the parsnip wine; but if you want to eat the parsnip slices afterwards, peeling is advised.

Cut into slices and place in a large saucepan. Add water until slices are covered.

Add thin peels of orange & lemon but be careful not to add any pith. (Or if you're going to be using citric acid instead, obviously omit this step).

Bring to the boil and then simmer for not more than 10 minutes, otherwise this will later cause the wine to be cloudy.

Strain the liquid into a fermentation vessel containing the sugar.

Add the juice of the orange and lemon. (Or citric acid).

Stir until the sugar is dissolved.

Top up with cold water until you have 4.5 litres of liquid.

Measure the initial Specific Gravity and note the reading. If you're after a decent strength wine of say 12% ABV, you may add more sugar in order to obtain a Specific Gravity reading of around 1.092. (Yes, you'll need a hydrometer for this.)

Add pectic enzyme, vitamin B1 tablet and yeast nutrient.

Add a brewing belt if necessary to keep the yeast at an ideal temperature for fermentation (around 20 degrees should be fine).

Add yeast and ferment for 4 days, stirring daily.

After 4 days, rack the wine into another vessel and fit an airlock.

When fermentation ends, measure the Specific Gravity again (it should be around 1.006).

Add 1 campden tablet per 4.5 litres.

Bottle and keep for 6 months before drinking.

Now, after you've boiled the parsnip slices, don't throw them away! They can still be eaten. In fact, when we made the first batch of wine, LSS made a rather good supper dish out of them, so here's her recipe for that:

Parsagne (Parsnip Lasagne) Recipe:

Firstly, you'll need a Bolognese sauce, and a white sauce.

Bolognese sauce: Ingredients:

- 500g minced meat

- 2 onions, chopped

- 200g tomato sauce (not ketchup, but a sauce made from diced tomatoes, onions and herbs)

- Stock cube (don't add any water, just add it to the mix)

- Salt and pepper, and your choice of herbs e.g. *herbes de Provence*

Method:

Fry the onions, then add the mince.

Once browned, add the rest of the ingredients and cook on low heat for half an hour or until the sauce is thick enough.

You can also add corn flour to thicken the sauce if necessary.

White sauce: Ingredients:

- 500ml milk

- 50g butter

- 3 tablespoons flour

- Salt and pepper

Method:

Melt the butter in a pan. Add the flour and stir well.

Add milk gradually, stirring constantly until a creamy consistency is achieved.

Add salt and pepper. (You can also add a little nutmeg for extra taste).

Now it's time to put everything together!

Ingredients:

- Parsnip slices left over from parsnip wine (you probably won't use all of them, so use the largest ones first)

- Bolognese sauce

- White sauce

- 100g grated Gruyère or cheddar cheese

Method:

In a buttered dish, place a layer of the parsnip slices. Overlap these so as to leave as few gaps as possible.

Then add a layer of Bolognese sauce.

Add a layer of white sauce.

Repeat the layering again – parsnips, Bolognese, white sauce; but keep a little white sauce in reserve.

Finish with a layer of parsnip slices and then cover the whole lot with the reserved white sauce.

Finally sprinkle the grated cheese over the top.

Place in the oven on a medium heat for about half an hour. (This is just to melt and toast the cheese; all the ingredients are already cooked). When the cheese is golden, it's done!

Serve with a nice salad and some home-brewed parsnip wine [7]and enjoy!

---

[7]Or home-brewed beer if your parsnip wine is not yet ready.

The La Darnoire website has been updated. Technology constantly advances, and the most recent iteration of the web site "language" is HTML5. So everything had to be changed to accommodate this. The update is now complete; and I took the opportunity to add some more content as well. In other Internet-related matters, Google has been annoying me; they deleted my motorcycle blog because their automated system considered it to be spam. The blog has been online for years. I requested a review; they apologised, and re-instated it. Then they deleted it again. So I have now given up on using Google's Blogger service and instead moved that one to self-hosted WordPress as well.

On other technological matters, so far we've been lucky with our phone/Internet connection. The Internet speed is bearable considering we're in the middle of nowhere. And we're actually the envy of T&M because we have a 1.5Mbps connection – they only have 750kbps. However, when the line was installed, in order to have a connection to the Internet, we were given a "*degroupage*" bundle. This means it's not an ordinary telephone line, but purely digital. In other words, we have what is known as an Internet telephone. So if there's a power cut – which happens a couple of times a year – the phone is completely dead. Of course this means things could get interesting if we need to telephone the emergency services during a power outage. Mobile phone reception here is dreadful.

We recently had a visit from neighbour J's cousin. He hadn't seen LSS since 1985, had heard she was back in town, and wanted to catch up. He's really into genealogy, and gave

LSS an unexpected present: his research on her family name which he had managed to trace back as far as 1655. This is not as strange as it sounds, as their families are related.

He's also somewhat of a buff regarding local history, and gave us some interesting photocopies of some of his research. During the Second World War there was a German radar station based on the farm next to neighbour J. It formed part of a network covering France, and was devastatingly reliable at detecting Allied aircraft. The electricity supply came all the way from Lamotte Beuvron, some 8km away, and was installed by Russian prisoners of war. It crossed La Darnoire and the farm of the Aged FIL. Of course no trace is left today; I suspect the cabling was supported by wooden posts.

Then, in July 1944, the electricity supply line was bombed and destroyed by two RAF De Havilland Mosquito's. In addition to bombs, they also jettisoned their long-range fuel tanks, and this chap's father promptly took one of them for use on his farm.

The radar station itself had a 7.5 metre dish, and was blown up by the departing Germans on the 20th August 1944. The radar dish was made of aluminium, and this was rapidly scavenged by the locals. In fact there are bits of it still in use here today, having been made into handy carrying baskets. The aluminium is of good quality, and quite thick.

The concrete base of the radar station is apparently still there, overgrown with trees. We must go and have a look, one of these days. I know there were the ruins of a German-constructed building in a field next to the road approaching the Aged FIL, probably about 200 metres from the site of the radar. It can still be seen on Google Earth, but not for long; the foundations were unfortunately removed last year by the Aged FIL's neighbour so that he could have unrestricted access with his plough. Perhaps one of these days I'll ask him if I can take a walk around the area with my metal detector.

M&O also paid us a visit, delivering a large, heavy, black plastic dustbin-bag. They had had the last hunt of the season on the property, and had bagged yet another wild boar; this was our share of the spoils. It included the boar's head, which LSS will turn into pâté. Both she and the Aged Aunt like it. I give it a miss, as I'm not too keen on the gelatinous texture. Our freezer is now practically full. As the Aged FIL does not like the taste of game, in previous years the hunters learned not to give him a share of their results. However, they seemed delighted to discover that we *do* like the taste of game, so they appear to be making up for lost time. We're certainly not complaining; it's saving us a fortune in shopping bills.

So how is the Aged FIL getting on? Well, his status is pretty much unchanged. He spends most of his time in bed, staring at the ceiling. Except for mealtimes, of course. Mind you, he's not quite as crotchety these days as he used to be. We nearly fell over with surprise last week – he asked if I could replace the current shallow step at the kitchen door with a small concrete ramp. This would enable him to wheel himself outside in his wheelchair. So as soon as the weather warms up enough for concrete to set properly, I will.[8]

---

[8] Once the weather had warmed up, he changed his mind; saying he'd rather stay in bed after all.

The kitchen woodstove has started smoking whenever there's a gust of wind from the west; so in between showers of rain, I fetched the double ladder, leaned it against the kitchen wall, and climbed up to the top to have a look at the rotating cowl on top of the chimney. It appears to be home-made – probably by the Aged FIL – and the problem is that the support bracket has rusted through and sagged, so the cowl itself is now off-centre and no longer rotates fully. It is binding on the side of the chimney pipe. I removed it, and this seems to have cured the smoking problem. I'll need to make another support bracket; one more item for the "To Do" list. We also had a storm recently, which deposited a layer of hail. This blocked one of the gutters so I had to go out in the downpour to clear it. I was not a Happy Bunny.

Wildlife diary: Mr and Mrs Duck have returned to the pond. We're not sure if it's the same female as last year, but in all likelihood it is. After all, last year's duck successfully raised a brood of eleven ducklings.

Also, a pair of blue tits have decided they want to come into the house, presumably wanting to make a nest somewhere dry after all this rain. They fly onto the window sill, or cling precariously to the wall at the side of the window, then flutter around in front of the glass. Getting tired of this, they perch on the bottom of the PVC window frame and peck hopefully at the glass as though they're knocking to come in. Taptaptaptaptap. Taptaptaptaptap.

But irritatingly, when you go over to open the window and say "Yes? What do you want?" they fly away. The down-side of this charming behaviour is that we now have muddy kitty paw-prints all over the inside of the window glass, as Cat could not fail to notice their behaviour. "Ooooh, yes, come in, do. Home Food Delivery, now that's what I call service."

March

ELECTRICAL issues occur at the Aged FIL. The polytunnel is completed, and construction starts on a garden shed and the solar thermal panel. The Renault 5 has more mechanical issues, and we vote in the local elections.

LSS has caught a cold, and unselfishly shared it with me. It's not too surprising, considering all the cold and damp weather we've had recently. But just to make up for it, a strange, warm, orange orb appeared in the sky, where it stayed all day long without a cloud in sight. Yes, the sun finally made an appearance!

I took advantage of the warmth to finish the fabrication of the polytunnel door, which, surprisingly, actually fitted in the frame. I must have measured it correctly. I had to scrape away some of the earth in front of it though; otherwise it would not have been able to open. A final remaining task regarding the polytunnel is to fix some mouldings to the inside of the door-frame to keep the end wall plastic taut, and then the keys can be handed over to LSS. She has already turned over some of the earth inside, ready to receive this year's first batch of lettuces and radishes.

Some brackets have been affixed to the lounge wall, ready for the installation of a wooden shelf (as soon as LSS has varnished it, that is). We'll then be able to move some of our books and work-related files out of the bedroom.

Another little project which was completed was the installation of a garden gate. I removed the Aged FIL's contraption of wonky fence posts and chicken wire, and instead re-purposed an old pallet. By sinking two stout timbers into the ground as gateposts, and mounting the pallet on a couple of hinges, we now have a very cottagey-looking garden gate. LSS painted it in the late afternoon sunshine, and very nice it looks too. She has also scraped away most of the mud in the courtyard and driveway, replacing it with the remainder of the gravel left over from the reedbed construction. The entire place is achieving a very landscaped look!

I decided to start constructing a garden shed, because I'm going to need the space in my workshop for the solar panel fabrication. Currently the wood chipper resides in my workshop, taking up considerable room. A garden shed would also be useful for keeping the petrol-powered tiller and lawnmower out of the rain. At the moment we are having to cover them with builders bags – which need to be weighed down with bricks to prevent them from blowing away. (Builders bags are large sacks made from woven polypropylene; and the ones we have originally contained one tonne of fertilizer each. The Aged FIL used to buy it in bulk. They were discovered in the little outbuilding next to the workshop).

In keeping with the ambience of the place, I will be making the shed out of wooden pallets, with a corrugated iron roof. I have laid four pallets next to each other to form a large square, adjacent to the exterior wall of the workshop. These pallets will be covered with boards raided from the Aged FIL's stock of concrete formwork timbers. That should provide a solid floor for the garden equipment, not to mention all the various rakes and shovels. Otherwise you can be sure that sundry bits and pieces would be falling through the gaps in the pallets.

However, the shed construction ground to a screeching halt, because I need some decent-sized sleeve anchors. These are metal fixings for anchoring a wooden beam to brickwork, and will be used to support the corrugated iron roof. So I decided to see if I could find these items in the closest town rather than buying them online. I started up the Renault 5.

Well, I didn't get very far. A few kilometres down the road the engine started struggling, as though I was driving with my foot on the brake, and something smelled hot. I pulled over, and checked each wheel in turn. The front right wheel was very hot indeed. Having experienced a similar issue with the rear wheel of the Honda ST1100 motorcycle, I suspected the cause was a stuck disc brake calliper piston. If the piston gets stuck, the brake pads are unable to release their pressure on the disc. So I was forced to abandon the expedition, and limped home again.

Despite extensive research, I was unable to source a set of pistons and seals online. However, it was fairly easy to find an entire brake calliper, at a price I suspected was lower than that of a set of pistons and seals. So an Internet order has now been made, and yet another entry has been made on my "To Do" list.

Well, that's one vehicle out of action.

We don't want to use LSS's Hyundai for driving around the property, as we want to keep it in good condition! And it wasn't here anyway, as LSS was using it. Therefore the other vehicle in the family stable had to be used; the Aged FIL's Aged Citroen AX. Unfortunately this car has problems as well. If it's left standing for any amount of time (which it has been), the fuel pump is incapable of drawing fuel through to the engine.

The Aged FIL's solution to this was to disconnect the fuel line from the carburettor, and suspend a small two-litre moped petrol tank from the inside of the bonnet, connecting this to the carburettor with a length of rubber pipe. Once the engine started, this tank was then disconnected and the vehicle's fuel line rapidly reconnected. The resultant vacuum was then able to draw fuel through from the tank. The cause of the problem could well be a perforated membrane in the mechanical fuel pump, which is probably located in the fuel tank itself. I don't have the time to thoroughly investigate this, but by installing a Facet electric in-line fuel pump which I already had, I was able to eliminate the need for messing about with fuel lines and two-litre tanks.

The other problem this vehicle had was that the Aged FIL had allowed the brake fluid reservoir to run dry, so the brakes didn't work. I filled it with fresh fluid and bled all the brake lines, which resolved this issue.

Oh - and the sleeve anchors for the shed? I gave up, and ordered them online.

It's been a while since the Aged FIL had a problem with electricity. In fact LSS was commenting on this just the other day. Which was a case of speaking too soon.

She received a phone call from one of the carers, saying that the electricity supply wasn't working. To cut a long story short, I had to visit the aged FIL's house with my multimeter. It wasn't a fuse problem. Well, it was at first; one of the fuses had blown. These are the old-style ceramic type fuses, with two terminals around which you can wrap a piece of fuse wire of suitable thickness. Or, if you require the house to burn down, just use ordinary fencing wire. But when a new piece of fuse wire was inserted and the power turned on, the electricity tripped again, this time at the main circuit breaker. The fuse wire remained un-melted. It's possible the three-phase load circuits are unbalanced, but diagnosing which circuit is the problem one is proving to be a nightmare. I resolved the issue temporarily by moving one of his electric heaters to a different circuit. The whole house really needs re-wiring. But this is not going to happen during the aged FIL's ownership.[9]

We took a day off to visit Friend L. The building where she lives is being renovated, so there was a lot of oak timber which the owner was discarding. We took the trailer with us, and filled it up with this scrap wood. Perhaps some of the beams can be re-used for something else, although unfortunately each one is peppered with hundreds of nails. If not, I'm sure they can be used in the wood stove.

Friend L had also requested that I bring my chainsaw along, ostensibly to be used in case the beams were too long for the trailer. This was not the case; but we discovered she did have

---

[9]I was later proved wrong. A couple of months after this issue, the ancient electrical wiring did indeed cause a fire. Fortunately it was in the outbuilding used as a garage. Which completely burnt down.

an ulterior motive. On one of her bicycle trips along the Loire River she had spotted a dead tree which had a particularly attractive branch, and she asked me to cut the branch for her as it would make a fine didgeridoo. Yes, she is learning how to play this instrument! I tried to look as Official as possible, as though it were an everyday occurrence to take a chainsaw with one when strolling along the banks of a major river.

The sunbathing/fishing family groups seemed quite surprised, but nobody said anything. Perhaps my orange chainsaw helmet had something to do with it.

This month heralds the start of Year Three!

So here's a brief update:

The coypu skin has now been tanned and is lovely and soft. I just need to make a template and then the fur can be cut and sewn into the shape of a hat.

The solar thermal panel construction is progressing slowly; the framework is now complete and is ready for the installation of the metal backing plate and pipework. It would have been too impractical to have constructed the panel in situ on the roof, but of course this creates a new problem – how do we get it up there? Fortunately the Aged FIL's neighbour has offered the use of his hay bale lifting machine, so I think if I build in some suitable lifting attachment points this should do the job.

The few parsnips which remained in the garden have now been processed; I now have fifteen litres of fermenting parsnip wine.

And as for the barn, work has finally started in this area. LSS freed up a quarter of the floor space by tidying up all the scattered cardboard boxes left over from our house move. These are all still full; there's a lot of stuff for which we don't yet have room, including an entire library of books. LSS then volunteered to start digging up the dirt floor. The hard-packed earth needs to be removed to a depth of about 20cm.

All the excavated soil will be re-used to fill in the erosion at the banks of the pond. And no, we're not done with the pond yet!

The plan for the barn floor is to put down a thin layer of lime to absorb any moisture, followed by a layer of compacted coarse gravel. Of course we didn't have enough gravel left over from the reedbed construction, so we had another ten tons delivered. Some sort of membrane will possibly then go on top of this layer, followed by lime concrete. I am going to have to mix this by hand; we can't get an entire truckload of ready-mixed concrete delivered, because we want to use lime, not cement, and concrete-mixing companies don't supply this. I still haven't tested the cement mixer attachment for the tractor. If I'm not happy with it, we may need to buy an electric mixer.

Then once the first quarter of the floor has been laid, we can start constructing a proper bathroom. With real walls, not army groundsheets!

There were two large piles of branches which had been stacked in a field before we obtained the wood chipper, and due to the growth of grass and brambles, these proved impossible to separate and feed into the chipper. We had two lovely bonfires instead. Of course now that we have the wood chipper we're being more careful where and how we stack any further branches. The wood chips we produce are either used for mulching in the garden, or placed under the chicken roosts where they can absorb a layer of chicken droppings before being added to the compost heap.

And we also discovered another of the late MIL's hidden caches. We visited the barn at the other farmhouse in order to dismantle a block of six heavy pre-cast concrete rabbit cages and bring them back to La Darnoire with the transporter box on the tractor. Neighbour J had promised us a pregnant female rabbit in Spring, and as Spring is now here, we'd better start getting ready to receive it, together with its impending litter! I had already poured a lime concrete footing for these cages, and it's been drying out over the past few weeks. We had decided that the best location for the cages was behind the workshop. This will provide them with some sunshine in the morning, but they'll be sheltered from the afternoon heat.

Anyway, tucked behind one of these cages in a dark recess of the barn was a wooden box, containing nine bottles of wine.

Two of these were half empty because the corks had dried out; but the other six had foil caps, so still had all of their contents. The remaining bottle was some sort of champagne, because it had a champagne cork complete with wire cage. We have no idea what the contents of these bottles are, because the labels disintegrated a long time ago. But we'll open them one at a time. If they're no good, we won't drink them.

Back at La Darnoire, the rabbit cages were installed, and

we're now ready to receive Mrs. Bunny and her impending offspring.

It was also haircut day again recently. I cut LSS's hair, and she cut mine. Fortunately we both like short hair, so it's not as difficult as it sounds. Together we've saved a fortune on hairdresser/barber shop bills.

I also had my first experience of voting in French Elections. This particular election was local, for the selection of the Mayor and Village Council for the next four years. As I'm a resident, I'm allowed to vote in this election, so LSS and I went down to the local village hall. We fetched neighbour J on the way, as nobody else had offered to take her. The Aged FIL has signed a paper allowing LSS to vote on his behalf, as he is reluctant to leave his bed for any non-essential reason. Eating is an essential reason. For now.

Unlike in the UK where at the polling station you receive a piece of paper and mark your selected candidate/party with a cross, in France you receive a large envelope in the post, during the week before the election. This envelope contains sheets of paper. Each sheet contains a list of names. Two sets of different councillors = two lists. In a village like ours which has less than a thousand inhabitants, you can confuse the issue even further by mixing and matching – crossing lines through names which don't take your fancy, and adding others.

Upon entering the village hall, you encounter a table containing stacks of these identical pieces of paper. (So enlighten me, what was the point of posting them to you in the first

119

place?) You take a sheet from each stack, and also an official envelope boldly printed with the inscription "*République française*". You then enter one of the three temporary polling booths where you fold your chosen list of names and insert this into the envelope. The non-used list is then customarily dropped on the floor, left in the polling booth, or, in our case, taken home for fire-lighting purposes.

You then make your way to the middle of the hall, where three officials site behind a long trestle table. The first takes your voting card; or, in our case, a piece of paper signed by the Mayor stating that we're allowed to vote. Despite several requests, our official voting cards seem to have been lost in the post. The first official then passes your proof of voting rights to the second official. This second official only has one available hand, as the other appears to be permanently attached to the lever which opens a little flap on top of the transparent plastic ballot box.

The second official then studies the voting card or document, and reads out your name to the third official, who is in charge of: The Book. This volume is the village electoral roll. The third official looks up your name in the book, and then covers the relevant page with a carefully-positioned transparent piece of plastic with a hole in it. He passes you a pen, and you sign the book through this little aperture. I suppose this is to prevent people writing things like "Kilroy was 'ere" or "Up The Workers!" in inappropriate places.

Once you've signed, the second official leaps into action by pulling the lever and opening the little flap through which you drop your envelope. The instant your envelope passes through the aperture, he states in a loud voice "YOU HAVE VOTED!" just in case you were in any doubt.

You can then go and chat with the other villagers if you so wish. We're rather hoping the election result will be a change of mayor, but it doesn't look like it will happen – early results indicate that the same old councillors will be elected again.

After dropping neighbour J back at her farm, and having had the obligatory coffee, we visited T&M as I wanted to borrow some pipe sealant. After another obligatory coffee we returned home. I opened the little outbuilding which currently houses some of our gardening bits and pieces, as I needed some plant food for my bonsai. I had a surprise when I opened the fertilizer packet though. I was greeted by the sight of what I initially thought was a dead mouse. Upon further investigation, I realised it wasn't. It was actually a dormouse, who had decided that a packet of fertilizer was an ideal place for hibernation. I wrapped him in an old hand towel, and left him to finish his hibernation on top of the pile of wood in the woodshed, hopefully out of reach of the cat.

One Sunday next month we're off to Paris – fortunately an outer suburb, not the city centre – to visit one of LSS's cousins for lunch. I have driven through Paris, and can't say I enjoyed the experience. Even the ring road (*Périphérique*) can be a nightmare; traffic joins and leaves from both sides – and Heaven help you if you're in the wrong lane. So with a bit of luck we'll be able to get to LSS's cousin without encountering too much traffic.

Wildlife diary: A stoat, or weasel, bounding up and down in the long grass at the back of the pond. We only caught a glimpse; by the time I had focussed the binoculars it had disappeared.

By the way, here's an old one. What's the difference between a stoat and a weasel?

Well, a weasel is weasily wecognisable, but a stoat is stoatally different.

I'll get my coat.

April

ELECTRICAL issues continue at the Aged FIL. We get our first rabbit. Further tractor punctures are dealt with; and LSS is not happy when a lunch is delayed. I visit a dentist, and EDF manages to damage a ditch with a lorry.

With regard to the aforementioned rabbit cages, I found that I had to strengthen the floor of one of them with a steel bar; although the cages are made of reinforced concrete panels, the floor panels themselves are rather thin, and one had cracked down the middle and was sagging a bit. Once this wasy done, LSS went to Neighbour J and came back with Mood. She's a lovely pale beige colour, and seems to like her new home. Why is she called Mood? It's an acronym. Mother Of Our Dinners. But she doesn't seem to mind.[10]

I've also been sorting out my collection of drill bits. No, I don't collect them like stamps. That would be silly. You see, in the Aged FIL's workshop I found several small wooden boxes containing lots and lots of these items of varying sizes. As he is unlikely to be doing any further drilling, they have now been incorporated with my own lot. Unfortunately many of them have been clumsily sharpened on a grindstone, so they are no longer any good for drilling anything other than cheese. Actually I think they'd struggle if it was a particularly hard cheese. Anyway, amongst my sundry collection of tools is an

---

[10]Actually the name didn't last. She soon became simply "Mrs. Bunny".

electric drill bit sharpener, so this has been dusted off and is seeing good use.

The soil in the garden was recently tested again. The pH is still pretty much the same as when I first tested it, soon after we moved in: 6.5, so very slightly acidic. Nitrogen levels are low to medium, potassium is low, and the level of phosphorus has dropped to medium, so the huge quantities of super-phosphates which the Aged FIL had regularly applied have finally started to disappear. The weather has now warmed up somewhat, so LSS has once again been busy in the garden and has already planted the first row of potatoes. These have been covered with a long cloche made from off-cuts of the PVC sheeting from the polytunnel. Using some black PVC sheeting which she found, she has also created a raised bed for the strawberry plants. I believe this is called "plasticulture".

Unfortunately the tomato seeds which were sown in pots in the new polytunnel have refused to grow, so we're not too sure what the problem is. The pots have, however, already produced a generous crop of weeds. Radishes are doing fine though.

The solar thermal panel base has now been given a coat of bituminous paint (left over from a roof repair I did on our house in Reading), and I've cut two corrugated iron panels to the correct size and joined them together. Well, I say corrugated iron. They're actually aluminium. Which, due to its greater thermal conductivity, is just the right material to use for a solar thermal panel. They've also been painted black with high heat paint. Unfortunately I discovered that another length of copper tubing was required, because I miscalculated. I only had 20 metres of tubing, and needed another 8 metres. So a visit to BricoDepot was carried out to remedy this mistake.

Installation of this tubing was not without issues, though. Even though it's of the annealed variety – in other words it's supposedly easier to bend – I had no end of trouble forming smooth 180° bends without kinking the tube.

Lacking a professional pipe bender, another method of bending copper tube smoothly is to fill it with sand prior to bending it. Unfortunately when each tube is ten metres long, this is not really a viable option. So really I was left with no alternative but to solder two 90° elbows at the end of each run. A total of 56 elbows were required.

Next the panel needs to be glazed by re-using some large panes of window glass which were originally on the cabin of a combine harvester. This vehicle went to a scrapyard a long time ago; but the Aged FIL fortuitously kept a few bits and pieces including the cabin glass.

Last week I recovered an old portable forge at the Aged FIL's farm, repaired the handle, and gave it a coat of paint. It's a fairly useful item – a while ago I had visited T&M to use his forge in order to repair a lump hammer. Unsuccessfully, as it turned out; the head parted company with the handle again. Anyway, I no longer need to traipse round to T&M if I want to do any blacksmithing! The kitchen chimney top cowl needs repairing, and the best method of doing this is to bend a piece of steel into the correct shape. This is obviously easier to do if you have a forge. I knew my home-made charcoal would come in handy.

We decided to go with our neighbours T&M to the newly-opened equestrian Parc l'Alméria in Salbris, as the published program promised some interesting events including jousting. Entrance was free, and we watched some very heavily choreographed jousting with the "knights" using bamboo lances. But it was fairly entertaining, except for the commentator who, like most commentators we have heard here, seemed to love the sound of his own voice. He kept up a constant monologue describing, in minute detail, how King Arthur (in the red coat) was about to tackle and vanquish the treacherous Sir Lancelot (in the black coat).

King Arthur was, of course, ultimately victorious, despite Sir Lancelot attempting to attack when King Arthur's back was turned. Luckily for him he was warned by shouts from the crowd. Then it was time for lunch. This was when things started to go downhill.

We discovered that there was a ticketing system in place; one could not just go up to the restaurant counter and order a hot-dog. Instead one had to purchase a ticket from a distant ticket-booth first. And suddenly at this ticket booth there was a tremendous crowd.

After queuing for an hour and a half we finally reached the front; but until that point we had not seen a priced menu in evidence anywhere. It was only when we got to the counter that we found one. It was affixed the wrong-way-round to a glass door. This was evidently done on purpose, because the prices were exorbitant. The management obviously calculated that after a person had been waiting in line for over an hour, they were ravenously hungry and not likely to leave the park and take a two-minute drive into town for a proper sit-down meal.

In hindsight, this is exactly what we should have done. The menu offering was a baguette with either a spicy *merguez* sausage, or an ordinary *saucisse*. As all of us liked *merguez*, this was obviously our selection. Having purchased our tickets (*merguez* baguette with chips, €6.50, glass of beer €2.50, per person) we then made another unpleasant discovery.

Of course all the people who had been ahead of us in the queue had to have gone somewhere. Yes, you've guessed it. They were by now all queuing at the restaurant counter. A further hour elapsed before we reached the front, by which time LSS was simply fuming. Do not even attempt to speak to her when she is hungry.

The cherry on top was that, as we got to the counter, an announcement was made that they had run out of *merguez* sausages. So instead we were given a rather insipid ordinary *saucisse*. In a baguette. Without butter. Or any sauce whatsoever. And about twelve half-raw chips in a little plastic tub. Also without any sauce. Even the beer (€2.50, remember?) was ordinary Heineken. Which would have been fine, except for the quantity. The plastic cup held a mere 200 ml.

So, if you happen to visit this part of France, either:

a) stay away from the Parc l'Alméria, or

b) bring your own food and drink.

From now on that's exactly what we are going to do. And to be more specific; we are going to carry out option a) in its entirety, and if we go to any other event/market/fair in this country, we'll carry out option b).

Other than that, we saw some spectacular stunt horseriding (I believe these horses are trained to act in films) and some equally stunning birds of prey.

Unfortunately LSS remained in a bad mood for the rest of the day.

Dentists.

Now there's a word which usually strikes fear into the heart of man.

Well, today I had my first experience with a French dentist. A bit of background is necessary first though. When I was growing up, fluoride was an added component to the water supply in Namibia. So I don't know if it was due to this, proper brushing, or simply genetics, but the sum total of my dental treatment thus far in life has been two fillings. Unlike Neighbour J, I do have a toothbrush.

I have thus been fortunate in that I don't need to visit a dentist very often. The last one I attended in the UK turned out to be a South African, and very good he was too. However, for the past couple of months one of my back teeth has been a bit painful, so LSS duly made an appointment for me with her dentist. It transpired that one of my two fillings had cracked.

The woman dentist swiftly appraised my dentition, complimented me on the state of my teeth, and decided it should be a simple job to drill out the remains of the old filling and insert a new one. "I'm not going to bother with anaesthetic," she said, much to my surprise. "If it hurts too much we'll reconsider."

A loud whining noise then commenced, but I stopped when it was obvious she was not paying attention.

Thirty seconds later a new filling had been inserted. Total time spent in chair: five minutes. Another appointment has been made for the customary tooth polishing, after which I will be presented with the bill.

But all in all, it was not a bad experience. As a reward for my good behaviour, LSS took me to Bourges where we visited the Cathedral and took the requisite touristy photographs. We also met up with one of LSS's work colleagues as arranged, and had lunch with her and her husband. They're both English. Unfortunately they both share the same first name, which I found somewhat confusing. He's now an artisanal carpenter – and it transpired he's fluent in Latin, which I found fascinating. So, of course, I tasked him with coming up with a motto to go over the door at Château La Darnoire: I told him the phrase in English, and he came up with this gem:

Etiam si non insanires, hic te adiuvaret.

Obviously it's not possible to give a direct translation into a dead language. But the phrase I gave him?

You don't have to be mad to live here, but it helps.

The dreaded Trip To Paris to have lunch with one of LSS's cousins took place. Actually, it wasn't too bad. It transpired that she lives completely on the outskirts of Paris, well before you even get to the *Périphérique*; so traffic was not an issue. Her husband had just retired, and took great delight in showing me his garage, containing baskets and baskets of tools he picks up for next to nothing at car boot sales. He's currently occupied with repairing the front end of a car belonging to one of his sons. The vehicle had an unfortunate encounter with a kerb, breaking lots of bits underneath including the steering. I suspect speed contributed towards the damage.

He's also renovating the back of the house, creating a sun-room. They have done all the construction work on the house themselves; it was purchased as a bungalow, but now has upstairs bedrooms complete with the ubiquitous Velux roof windows. This work has taken some fifteen years, and the main stairs are still not finished, so I don't feel so bad about the slow progress of our own renovation work.

As they were aware that we did home brewing, (we took them a couple of 750ml bottles of beer), we came away with several boxes of empty champagne bottles they'd been collecting for us. They also gave us a large bag filled with stale bread for the hens.

The problem with the Renault 5's braking system has now been resolved. When I jacked the vehicle up and removed the wheel, I discovered that my initial diagnosis was correct; the brake calliper pistons had completely seized. I had purchased a complete re-manufactured calliper for around €40 including postage. All the vehicles are now once again operational.

And I finally completed the garden shed. A long plank of wood was fixed to the exterior of the workshop wall, using the sleeve anchors which I had purchased online from the UK. This plank of wood was then used to support that end of the corrugated iron roof. The walls themselves were also constructed from pallets, which I covered externally with more corrugated iron sheets, all courtesy of the Aged FIL's old woodshed. This ramshackle structure has gradually been collapsing, so I've been helping it along a bit. The wooden struts supporting the sagging roof are systematically being brought back here to join the firewood pile. At least now all our garden machinery can be stored out of the rain and no longer take up space in my workshop!

As it has become known locally that we have four free-range hens which are not fed on anything genetically modified, chemically altered, or full of pesticides, several persons have now applied to be put on the waiting list for purchasing eggs. We therefore need more hens, if we want to be able to eat any eggs ourselves. We originally planned to purchase an additional two hens annually in order to refresh the flock, but we've now reconsidered this schedule. So two new youngsters were duly fetched from the poultry supplier. According to Internet wisdom, they should be kept separate from the original four birds for a week, after which they can be put together so that the pecking order can be established. [11]

This month also sees the annual equestrian event in the nearby town of Lamotte Beuvron, which entails 10,000 horses visiting the area. No, that's not a misplaced comma. This means that people have a requirement for stabling, and as we have a vacant field available, we've decided to prepare it to

---

[11]We later found that this was unnecessary. Now we just add the youngsters straight away and let them sort themselves out.

receive horses. We'd come up with this idea earlier in the year. Or was it last year? Anyway, in preparation, LSS has cut the grass in the field with the tractor-mounted brush cutter. To provide water for the animals, we brought a heavy cast-iron bathtub from the other farm, where it once saw service as a cattle trough. We had to use the transport box on the tractor to bring it here; it would certainly not have fitted in the Renault 5!

I have been using a manual post-hole digger to install some stout fence-posts in this newly-named Horsey Field. These will serve as the supports for an electric fence. For reasons of clarity I should point out that Horsey Field lies on the other side of the communal dirt road which runs past the farmhouse. Earlier in the year I had already laid some conduit in a trench between the borehole and the road, prior to building the hen coop in this location.

Now this was the road which was a muddy soup last year. Upon complaining to the Mairie, a contractor turned up to repair it. Of course during this time there was torrential rain, which didn't make his job any easier. Anyway, it took several days, and one evening I took advantage of the contractor's absence – he'd finished for the day – to dig a trench across the road. Not strictly allowed, of course! I laid the conduit in the trench, which ended next to one of our chestnut trees, and then refilled it; marking each end of the trench with a brick. The following day the contractor returned and laid more gravel. He didn't notice the unauthorised additions to his work.

The next job will be to dig a trench for the conduit which will carry the water and electricity from the road into the field. I have decided against digging this one by hand; as the Aged FIL has a ditch-digging implement which fits on the tractor I thought I'd see if this ancient machine can be used.

So, bright and early the next day, we went over to the Aged FIL to get the tractor ready. But of course, nothing ever goes smoothly. The first problem was that, once again, one of the tractor's front wheels was flat. The tractor is obviously out of commission until I fix it.

There are actually two spare wheels, but we found that these were both flat as well! We brought the two spares back to La Darnoire where at least I have my tools handy, but I was unable to get one of the tyres off its rim; I need a bigger hammer. Or at least a tractor-sized bead breaker tool. The other spare wheel has what is known as a split rim. Basically the rim is in two parts so it's easier to remove the tyre. I successfully removed the tube.

Now, when I was a lad, I had a bicycle. And I frequently had to repair punctures. The source of the leak is generally found by putting some air into the inner tube and submerging it into a bucket of water to locate the hole. Fast forward to today, and the same principle applies. However, you can't fit a tractor inner tube into a bucket. However, we do have a bathtub; which, when not in use, resides in our front garden! I found that the problem was not actually a puncture, but a leaking valve. The valve interior thread has had it, so inserting a new Schrader valve had no effect. The valve housing itself needs to be replaced. Unfortunately because of the split-rim design, the brass valve housing – which, thank goodness, is replaceable – is about 10cm long, with two 45° bends in it. And of course that's just the type of valve we don't have!

Fortunately, later in the afternoon, LSS managed to find another punctured tube with a similar elongated valve in the dark recesses of the Aged FIL's workshop. I was able to use that valve to fix the split-rim tyre.

Once the repaired wheel had been installed, we attempted to hitch the ditch-digging attachment to the tractor. After several minutes of effort, this was finally attached; but then we couldn't find the drive-shaft. Of course the Aged FIL couldn't remember where he'd put it. After much searching, we eventually found it in a shed next to his workshop. However, as it had not been used for years, it needed the application of a stout metal pole as a lever in order to lengthen the telescopic section sufficiently to reach from the tractor's power take-off to the ditch-digger.

All of this malarkey meant that by the time everything was ready for actually digging ditches it was starting to get dark. I parked the tractor at La Darnoire ready for an early start the following day. I've also asked LSS to pick up a new 7.50×20 inner tube the next time she passes by the village's agricultural supplies company, because all the spare inner tubes we have found are very heavily patched.

The next day, an early start was made, and after a mere thirty minutes, the trench was complete. After returning the tractor to its shed, I then installed the conduit, fed the electricity cable and hosepipe through, and filled in the trench.

With the rate at which the grass grows, in a couple of months you won't be able to tell there was a trench there at all.

Towards the end of the month, Mrs Bunny started collecting straw from all over the cage and building a tunnel in one corner, so it looks like she's getting ready to have kittens. Why do they call baby rabbits kittens? No idea.

LSS has managed to break the petrol-engined weed-eater, so that's another item for the list of things to be repaired.

We have also now sampled our second bottle of home-made perry.

A month ago we had tried some, but it was very flat and a bit sharp. I'm pleased to report that bottle number 2 was much improved. It would appear that malo-lactic fermentation has started, so it was moderately bubbly and tasted much better, so we can chalk up another success on the home-brewing front! Speaking of home-brewing, the Aged FIL still has the legal right to make moonshine (home-distilled alcohol). Apparently this right was issued in the past to French farmers who served in the armed Forces. Unfortunately it's not hereditary, and I believe it's no longer being issued. So whilst the Aged FIL is still around, we've decided that this year we will gather a crop of pears and/or apples – depending on which is most abundant – and use his licence to have these distilled into a form of brandy. Purely for medicinal purposes, of course.

With the tractor's flat spare wheels now taking up room in my workshop, I turned my attention once again towards puncture repairs. As a remnant from my days of Land Rover ownership, I still have a Hi-Lift jack. In case you don't know what this is, it's also known as a farm jack, and consists of a stout steel perforated bar, with a ratchet mechanism and a sturdy handle attached. It can easily lift a tractor in order to change a wheel; can be used to pull fence posts out of the ground, or even as a manual winch. The addition of a fixed bracket to one end of the bar also means one can use it to compress things, although I've never used mine for this. Well, supposedly you can also use it as a tyre bead breaker.

Some investigation revealed that the method for doing this is to put the tyre underneath the front bumper of your Land Rover, place the base of the jack on the tyre, and jack up the vehicle. Well, I no longer have a Land Rover, and the tractor is at the other farmhouse, so obviously another method needed to be used. Considering the problem, I had an idea. I placed the tyre on the ground, put some blocks of wood on the surface of the tyre opposite each other, and a stout oak beam across these. A strong chain was attached to the underside of the rim in the centre, and by looping the chain over the lifting jaw of my Hi-Lift jack, I was soon rewarded by a loud "pop" as the tyre bead let go of the rim. Having repeated this procedure on the other side of the tyre, I removed the inner tube and inflated it.

Once again I made use of the bathtub in ortder to find the puncture, but did not see any escaping air bubbles. The valve was not leaking either, so I put the inflated inner tube to one side to see if it goes flat after a couple of days. The bead-breaking procedure needed to be repeated on the other spare wheel, but the afternoon was wearing on, and we had a dinner invitation.

This was with Lady A. (I suspect this will be a one-off occurrence, so I don't think she qualifies to be included in the list of cast members at the beginning of this book). This is one of LSS's adult students. Although she retired five years ago she decided she wanted to learn English because everyone else in her family is fairly fluent! Her husband is in the very top echelon of one of the largest companies in France, so they live in a residence which is known locally as a château. It's a very large converted hunting lodge. I refer to her as Lady A not because she has a title but simply to indicate the type of person she is.

Cook had prepared a dinner of asparagus, followed by roast beef, and a simple dessert of strawberries and ice cream. I have been to more formal dinners – notably in the army Officers' Mess – but this one qualified as being fairly formal. It was what is known as "butler service" in English (or "*service à la française*" in French!)

Lady A was very pleasant, although it was subtly evident that a large portion of her income had gone straight into the pockets of Parisian plastic surgeons. She mentioned that she was looking to buy another house in the south of France. Two of her grandchildren were staying with her for the school holidays, as the skiing season in Switzerland was over for the year. They attend school in Poland, so were fluent in Polish, French (obviously), and English. They are currently also studying German and Mandarin. Very well-mannered they were too. Lady A is keen to visit London towards the end of the year and wishes to employ LSS as an official translator for the trip.

Following this dinner, the telephone by our bed woke us at 1 a.m. No, it was not a telephone call. It was emitting desperate chirrups because there had been a power cut, and its batteries were running low. As soon as we were fully awake, it died completely, so we went back to sleep. Now, a bit of background is required; not only for the telephone, but for what happened next.

When we moved in, there was obviously no telephone installed. We contacted France Telecom (now Orange) and to cut a long story short, we finally had a telephone. However, it was not an ordinary telephone, but an Internet phone. In other words, if there's no electricity, there's no telephone either. So if there's a power cut during an emergency, we have to rely on mobile phones. And because we're in the middle of woodland, mobile phone reception is rather poor. Inside the house itself, it is pretty much non-existent. There is a mobile phone mast at Les Alicourts, the large holiday resort. This is some three kilometres away as the crow flies, but there are a lot of tall trees in the way, so this doesn't help.

The second part of the background information concerns the Aged FIL. First of all, his house has no central heating. Instead electric heaters are used, much to the delight of the electricity supply company shareholders. And as he has such a fear of falling down and not being able to get up again, we implemented something known as *"Présence Verte"*. This is a machine which is connected to his telephone, and is triggered by a push-button device he wears on his wrist. When he presses the button, he can talk to the control centre. The control centre then telephones four numbers in sequence: LSS's mobile, the telephone here, M&O, and then Mrs D (one of the carers). If no response is received from the first number, they try the second, and so on. If no response is received from any of the four numbers, they contact the fire brigade. The Aged FIL's telephone is an ordinary one, so it still works if there is a power cut.

So, on with the tale.

We were awoken again soon after 6 a.m. by the lights of a vehicle driving into our courtyard. It was M&O. Apparently the Aged FIL had pushed his button, and *Présence Verte* had swung into action. There was no response from LSS's mobile, which was in its customary place on the kitchen table, but, as usual, not receiving a signal. There was no response from the telephone here, which was out of action due to the power cut. Fortunately M&O had sleepily responded to the call. However, they had been unable to gain access to the Aged FIL's house because the door was locked. This is usually the case at night. So they came here. LSS explained about the telephones, and assured them she would investigate whatever problem it was that had caused the Aged FIL to push his button. Slightly disgruntled, M&O went back home. Fortunately this sort of thing has not been a frequent occurrence; it is only the second time in two years they've had to respond.

LSS jumped into the car and drove off to the Aged FIL.

It transpired that he had pushed his emergency button because there really was an emergency.

His electric heaters had stopped working.

Instead of hitting him over the head with a bat, LSS explained that there had been a power cut, and that we were

139

without power as well. The silly thing is: on one occasion during the previous week the carer had not turned up to get him out of bed and feed him breakfast. Not remembering that he had an emergency button to press, he had simply laid there waiting until lunchtime.

Whilst at his house, LSS used his telephone to call Neighbour J; she was without power as well. ERDF – the French electricity supply company – was then contacted, and they said they were aware of the problem.

They explained that a possible lightning strike to a substation had downed part of the local grid, and they were investigating.

Whilst LSS was away, I noticed an ERDF van drive past our house. Later in the morning the van returned and the driver asked if there were any overhead pylons on the property. I replied in the affirmative and told him he was welcome to use the private access road between us and the Aged FIL to inspect them. He thanked me and drove away. I didn't think my French was that bad!

After lunch, I walked to the post-box to see if there was any mail. I discovered that one of the ERDF Iveco lorries had buried itself in the ditch near the post-box. It had driven along the farm track towards us, before the driver seemingly changed his mind and decided to reverse back again. Which was a mistake; because the road curves slightly at that point. The right-hand rear wheels had slid into the metre-deep ditch, and the right-hand front wheel had followed suit. The chassis was resting gently on the edge of the ditch. Because there was now no traction for the left-hand wheels, these had just spun without doing any work, as evidenced by the gouge marks both front and rear tyres had left in the road surface. The driver was nowhere to be seen. I went back and fetched LSS and the camera.

Upon my return, I noticed something which the driver hadn't. On the front bumper was a brand new, cellophane-wrapped, unused winch.

Now I'm pretty sure I could have extracted the lorry from the ditch under its own power by using a combination of the winch and diff-lock. Perhaps ERDF drivers should participate in a Land Rover off-road event as part of their training.

Later that afternoon the recovery vehicles arrived. These consisted of a beefy recovery truck, and a large crane. Unfortunately I was busy at the time doing something else, but LSS wandered down with the camera and watched the recovery.

The power finally came back on here at around 3 p.m. LSS went to the Aged FIL to check on the status of his power supply, and discovered that he was still without electricity. Yet another call to ERDF revealed that the case had been marked as resolved, and the technicians were on their way back to Blois. The control centre promised that they would be recalled, and his power was finally restored by 5 p.m.

I think we need to purchase a generator; we're pretty self-sufficient in everything except electricity, which is needed to power the borehole pump and our two freezers – not to mention the telephone!

As the electricity was working once again, the following day was spent installing the electric fence in Horsey Field. We had purchased the plastic fence posts and electric fence tape from the UK, as it was cheaper than buying it here, even with the postage. The Aged FIL has three electric fence energizers, so at least we didn't have to buy any of these. Afterwards I strolled along the fence line with my new electric fence tester, and found that I had indeed connected everything up correctly; the voltage is at least 5,500V throughout. I then connected up the hosepipe which will feed the old cast-iron bath in the field, and am pleased to report everything is now ready to receive paying guests! Ah, if only!

LSS telephoned the Mairie to report the damage to the road and ditch caused by the ERDF incident. The village *garde champêtre* (a combination of a forest ranger, game warden and police officer) turned up with a solution: two sticks and a roll of warning tape, with which he cordoned off the damaged area. Fortunately there is still just enough space on the roadway to get past in a vehicle, although this does mean driving partially in the field opposite the ditch.[12]

Some parcels also arrived in the post. Well, I say arrived. They actually had to be fetched from the local village Post Office; but more on that in a moment. These parcels included some parts which I'd ordered online for the weed-trimmer repair, so it's now operational once again. In between some showers of rain, I tested it by clearing the jungle of weeds around the chicken coop, and also tidied up around the bore-hole. I think I may have to put down some sheets of plastic

---

[12]The damaged road and ditch were repaired several months later.

covered with gravel in order to keep the weeds at bay in this area.

So, I mentioned the village Post Office. With regard to the mail, we've recently experienced problems. You see, when we moved in, we inherited a very helpful postman. He very quickly found out – for himself – where we lived in relation to our post-box. That sounds odd. But if you consider that our house is some 400m away from our post-box, down a farm track, that may make the scenario easier to understand. Anyway, he took great delight in delivering any large parcels, or those which needed to be signed for, because this meant he could usually have a bit of a chin-wag – especially once he found out we'd come here from Britain, which he likes. He always had a smile on his face, so it was a pleasant experience to receive any mail. On the odd occasion that neither LSS nor I were here, he always left the parcel in the (unlocked) Renault 5 out of the rain; obviously signing for it himself. As I said, a very helpful chap.

However, he has been absent recently. In fact, he appears to have been replaced by another postie. This woman still doesn't know (or perhaps it's simply that she doesn't care) where we live, despite our having typed out some directions which we affixed to our mailbox: "La Darnoire is 400m further down the road". So nowadays we get lots of "Sorry we were unable to deliver your parcel because you were out" cards left in the post-box – despite my being here all the time. In fact, when I'm expecting a delivery, I arrange to be either indoors or in my workshop rather than out and about cutting firewood. So these missed deliveries inevitably mean one of us has to go to the village the following day to collect the undelivered parcels.

Well, LSS was speaking to someone in the village the other day, who reported that the reason we no longer had Mr. Nice Postman was because he had been in a vehicle accident.

A few days later we happened to visit Neighbour J for something-or-other, and mentioned the matter. She has the same post(wo)man, and also happens to be the font of all local knowledge. "Oh no," she exclaimed. "He didn't have an accident. Well, he did, but it wasn't serious. He passed out at the wheel and drove into a ditch. He wasn't hurt. But he was booked off sick to have some tests done at the hospital. And they've discovered that he has cancer."

So he won't be resuming his mail-delivering duties. Instead we've heard he's been given another job at the main Post Office. But sad as this may be, this is not the problem. If he had simply been replaced by another postie, that would have been fine as far as the postal deliveries were concerned. The new postie could have learned where we were, and all would have been tickety-boo. But no. The way things work in France is that if you're on long-term sick leave, your position is not filled by someone permanent. Even if you're going to be booked off sick until such time as you retire, or if you're given a different job. Instead, what they do is hire someone who's registered at the local *Pôle emploi* (Job Centre). This is generally someone who has been unable to find any other job, and they are offered a temporary three-month contract with the post office. Take it, or lose your benefit payments.

So we are now getting a lot of different posties, generally women. As they are only temporary, they have no inclination to learn the details of their routes. So the "Sorry you were out" cards seem to be destined to be left in our mailbox for the considerable future.

Anyway, that's enough about the French Postal System for now.

As I was in a repairing mood I also fixed my orbital sander by replacing the bottom bearing which had seized. And LSS popped in to the Equestrian Federation in Lamotte Beuvron to tell them our Horsey Field was available for hire.

A day or so later, with yet another heavy rainstorm taking place, I discovered the rainwater recovery system barrels were overflowing. Investigation revealed that the inlets to the two end barrels had become clogged with debris from the gutters, so water was not reaching the overflow pipe in the final barrel. I had originally installed leaf traps in the gutter downpipes, but found that these became blocked very rapidly, so I removed them. This was probably not a good idea.

Anyway, I have an old Vax wet-and-dry vacuum cleaner which I normally use for dust extraction for the radial arm saw in my workshop. Once the rain had stopped, I emptied most of the water in the clogged barrels into the garden, and used the vacuum cleaner to clear out the debris from the bottom. The overflow system is once again working. I'm really impressed with this vacuum cleaner; it's about 20 years old and still working fine.

Wildlife diary: Once again, a somewhat unexpected encounter. I went to water my bonsai; and although the watering can was full of water, nothing was coming out of the spout. So I peered in, and nearly dropped the can in surprise when I saw a little face peering back at me from the spout. It's a good job we have several watering cans, because this one is now out of commission! Its occupant is a tree frog, *Hyla arborea*.

Mrs. Duck returned to the pond once again, and made a nest containing ten eggs. Unfortunately a few days later LSS happened to go past when Mrs. Duck was absent, and reported that there were now only three eggs. Mrs. Duck took up residence again a few minutes later. The following day there were no eggs left. Mrs. Duck has disappeared as well. We think it's unlikely to have been a fox; but a marten could have been the culprit, as we have seen one around here.

May

NOT only are there further electrical issues at the Aged FIL, but the old wiring finally causes a fire. Yet more tractor punctures occur. The baby rabbits arrive, and the solar thermal panel nears completion. And we discover a coypu in our pond.

The first of May was yet another bank holiday. May is known for bank holidays in France! LSS managed to talk her Aged Aunt and Uncle into coming around for lunch. They're both 82, and the Aged Aunt is starting to suffer from Alzheimer's. I think they enjoyed the visit, although I don't think they quite understood our explanation of the Thermal Store for hot water, and the Greywater Reedbed for waste-water treatment.

And as it was the first of the month, it was time for the cat to have her monthly anti-flea and anti-tick treatment, namely Frontline. This is horribly expensive here, so we buy it online from Australia. Well, I just examined the packet. Guess where it's made? France. Something's very wrong when you can buy a product which has been shipped to the opposite side of the globe and back more cheaply than buying it where it's made...

Mrs. Bunny started pulling out clumps of her fur and packing it neatly in the straw in one corner of the hutch, so it looks like we'll soon have little bunnies.

LSS opened another recently-discovered pot of preserves from the late MIL. This time it was cherries; dated 1997. They were still edible though.

We are now collecting 6 eggs per day, as the two young hens have also begun production. But yet another person has joined the waiting list, so now we need yet another two hens! We went with T&M to visit the farm fair in Souvigny-en-Sologne to see if there were any suitable birds, but the only decent specimens we saw were a lot more expensive than those at our local poultry farm, so it looks like we'll be getting two from the same place we bought the others. Which is fine, because we haven't had any problems with them so far. Apart from the one we call "Fatty" who has a tendency to lay her eggs at night from her perch. Fortunately we now have some fairly thick straw underneath so they are normally unbroken. I suspect Fatty could well be the first of our hens to meet Mr. *Le Creuset* (a brand of cast-iron cookware).

A few days later we did buy another two hens; that makes a total of eight. Well, we have the room. Of course putting the new occupants to bed was interesting; they'd never seen a perch before! Unfortunately this means the hens' profit and loss account is in the red again, but I calculate we only need another 35 eggs to reach the new break-even point.

T&M then invited us to join them for a barbecue. We spent an enjoyable afternoon as their neighbours came over as well. When we returned home, we discovered that Mrs. Bunny had given birth. Although it was difficult to make an accurate count because of all the wriggling, it would appear that there are seven or eight little bunnies. They're all dark grey, and emitting high-pitched squeaks. Mrs. Bunny is consuming vast quantities of food. We haven't actually bought any rabbit food; she has some barley – courtesy of the hens' food supply – and particularly likes clumps of grass. She is also eating kitchen vegetable scraps, although she is not very fond of leeks. As the late MIL kept rabbits, LSS is fairly expert on which plants to feed rabbits, and there's a lot of rabbit food growing wild around the place!

LSS managed to sell one of the old agricultural tractor attachments for which we have no use, and the purchaser came to collect it today. Unfortunately whilst we were connecting the plough-type thing to his tractor, I noticed that the front tyre of the Aged FIL's tractor was, once again, flat.

As I had already managed to break the bead on one of the spare tyres, in the afternoon I inserted the new inner tube which LSS had picked up last week, and yet again changed the tyre on the tractor. We'll see if it goes flat again this weekend. I think the Aged FIL must be getting out of bed in the middle of the night, visiting the tractor shed in his wheelchair, and letting the air out. You couldn't call it sleepwalking though. Perhaps sleepwheelchairing?

We had an unexpected visit from Friend L; she had left her village on May 1st on her bicycle to take a scenic camping tour along the Loire River. She stayed for lunch and then headed home.

As planned, I laid some sheets of polythene around the borehole, and covered these with a layer of gravel; hopefully this will keep at least some of the weeds in check. I also took advantage of the sunshine to cut some more wood for the woodshed. Several weeks ago I had recovered several large branches which had been brought down by some high winds, and these had been stacked near the saw-horse waiting for a day when it wasn't actually raining. Once this lot are dealt with, I intend recovering some more from the Aged FIL's farm.

I have now completed the soldering of the tubes for the solar panel. I connected it temporarily to the Horsey Field water supply pressure vessel with a hosepipe, in order to test for leaks. I don't want to install it on the roof and then find it's dripping! The Horsey Field tank holds some 300 litres of water at 4 bars pressure, so this is four times the pressure required by the solar collector when in operation. When installed, the solar collector will contain propylene glycol at a mere 1 bar, as it will be an open vented system.

I was pleased to find that there were no leaks, so it would appear my joint soldering was up to scratch. The pipework was then fixed to the backing plate by using lengths of copper wire salvaged from the old electric wiring I ripped out when I upgraded the household electricity. I then fixed the temperature sensor in place using thermal glue. Once that was done, the copper tubing received two coats of matt black paint.

It's important to paint everything black as this absorbs the most solar energy. Matt black is a better choice because a gloss paint is more reflective. I had originally intended drilling holes through the roof tiles to mount the panel; but after a bit of careful thought I have instead opted to make some brackets. These will be fixed to the rafters, and by following the contour of the tile, no drilling will be necessary. Of course this means I needed to pay a visit to the Aged FIL's workshop to see if there was any suitable scrap metal. I think the panel itself will need a bit of reinforcing on the underside, as the plywood box seems a bit flimsy. Once it's in place it should be fine, but I don't want it to fall apart as it's being hoisted onto the roof!

I fitted the backing plate, complete with tubing, into the plywood frame, having first inserted a layer of glass fibre for insulation. Now I just need to drill some holes in the end of the frame where the tubes will exit, and then the panes of glass can be installed.

Having visited the Aged FIL's workshop, a slight change of plan was made. I didn't find any bits of scrap metal to make brackets, but I found some longer pieces which were ideal to make a frame, large enough for the solar panel to fit into. This then had to be fixed to the roof, of course. But before that could be done, it needed a couple of coats of paint!

Once this paint had dried, I set up the scaffolding and roof ladder, and attached the frame to the roof by using lengths of builders' band. This is a very versatile invention; and sees a multitude of uses. If you've never heard of builders' band, no, it's not a musical group. It's a roll of galvanized perforated steel tape, usually around 1mm thick. And although I no longer have a tremendous fear of heights – which was cured by doing some skydiving during my university years – I didn't feel very comfortable up on the steeply-pitched roof; and work was somewhat limited as one hand was occupied with clinging to the ladder! I therefore needed to devise some sort of safety harness.

This was achieved by using a thick polypropylene Land Rover tow-rope with a shackle. I clipped the shackle to the roof ladder; and the eye at the other end of the tow- rope was threaded through a shorter length of rope, still in my possession from my army days; it's called a "*Tokkel Tou*" (utility rope). This was fastened around my waist. Well, it was better than nothing, and I felt a lot safer! I then had two hands available for the job.

The solar panel will simply rest inside this frame and will be fixed to it with screws.

The hens then laid a new record number of eggs; eight! Well, actually seven, because one was broken; I don't think the newest hens had been getting enough calcium. So they were given an additional ration of crushed oyster shells, and they have been pecking at this as though their lives depended on it.

And once again, the tractor's front tyre is flat. And it's the one with the new inner tube! I don't understand it at all. I had carefully checked inside the tyre for any protruding thorns when I installed the new tube and found nothing. It's a conspiracy. Or, the Aged FIL is indeed getting out of bed at night and letting the air out.

So off we went to the Aged FIL so that I could pump up the three spare tractor tubes using the ancient three-phase home-made compressor in his garage. In reality, I think the reason the tubes are going flat is not because the Aged FIL is getting out of bed in the middle of the night to let the air out, but that they do actually have punctures. On further reflection, I suspected that when testing for leaks I had not inflated them sufficiently. This time, having pumped them up fully, I found that my suspicions were correct. Each one had a tiny puncture. All of these holes have now been patched, and I asked LSS to feel around the inside of the actual tyres to see if there are any thorns, as her hands are more sensitive than mine. I couldn't feel anything, but there must have been a thorn through the casing somewhere. But she didn't find any either.

I returned to the dentist for my second scheduled appointment. The bill came to a grand total of €62, which to my mind is incredibly cheap when I compare it to the cost of dentistry in the UK, which is where I last attended a dentist for a check-up. Apparently in France the government has set a fixed tariff for things like fillings. Supposedly one should have a dental check-up every six months. I'll try and compromise, and make an entry in my calendar for the next visit. Perhaps in two years' time.

We also visited Neighbour J to pick elderflowers, for this year's batch of elderflower champagne and elderflower cordial.

Later in the month the two newest hens were allowed to exit their quarantine area to join the others. They are now roosting with their older companions so they've figured out how things work!

We have decided to close my bank account and convert LSS's bank account into a joint account. The reason for this is twofold. In the UK, banking is free. In France, you're charged a monthly fee of approximately €8.50 just for the privilege of having a bank account. By having a single joint account, we're saving one of these monthly fees. Also, my nearest HSBC branch in Brinon has now closed, and the banking facilities have been moved to a town called Argent-sur-Sauldre, several kilometres beyond Brinon. As LSS is the one who tends to do the shopping, and is the one currently receiving payments for giving English lessons, it makes sense that her account is the one to be kept.

LSS called HSBC on my behalf. (I can cope fine with French when face-to-face with someone, but find conversing in French on the telephone difficult.) She asked what they required in order to close my account. They replied that all they needed was a letter signed by me.

"What about the chequebook and bank cards?" LSS asked.

"Oh no, we don't need those back. Once the account is closed you can destroy them."

We are by now, of course, thoroughly suspicious of any official information received; due to the fiasco of the *Quittus Fiscal* paperwork in our first year of residence – for further details, read "A Bathtub in Our Garden"!

So LSS drafted a letter for me, requesting HSBC to close my account. It will be posted on Monday by recorded delivery.

Now, if you remember correctly, I have mentioned several times in the past that the Aged FIL's house is in dire need of electrical rewiring. However, every time the subject has arisen, he has refused, saying that:

a) he does not have the money. "If the house needs rewiring, YOU can pay for it. I'm not paying a cent!" and

b) it's not necessary anyway. "It's worked fine since the electricity was first installed in 1946. I don't care if standards HAVE changed since then."

154

Actually it hasn't worked fine. I've lost count of the number of times our telephone has rung because his electricity supply has tripped due to yet another blown ceramic fuse.

Well, this Saturday was the day that our predictions came partially true.

At 6 p.m. LSS received a phone call from one of the carers. "I've just arrived to give him his dinner, and I've called the Fire Brigade; the garage is burning down."

We dropped everything and dashed over. The Fire Brigade arrived some ten minutes later. The reason for the delay was that the village fire engine is apparently in for repair, so they had to enlist the help of the next village, Brinon. By now the entire building had collapsed, with the exception of one gable end which was still standing forlornly amongst smouldering roof timbers. Of course the fact that one wall had been slightly bent in the past due to the Aged FIL reversing into it with the tractor had not helped the situation. Buried underneath the rubble were the compressor, welding machine, drill press, and heavy-duty lathe. Fortunately we had removed the Aged FIL's car from the garage several months ago, as it was getting covered in owl droppings.

The police were there as well. Apparently when there's a fire, they have to attend, in order to determine whether the cause was accidental, or arson. The mayor turned up too, as did the *garde champêtre*. The reason THEY attended was because it was a domestic fire, and they needed to ascertain whether the occupants would require re-homing if the building turned out to be uninhabitable. Rather a good system, I think.

Either that or they just liked some good drama. And then the fire brigade had called EDF, the electricity supply company; so that was yet another vehicle clogging up the Aged FIL's access road. The fire brigade had wanted to ensure that when they sprayed the smouldering roof beams with water, there were no unpleasant electrical surprises.

In discussion with the fire brigade, it seemed that the cause of the fire was : (wait for it)...

... the ancient wiring, which had finally given up the ghost. Fortunately the ancient ceramic fuses had given way as well, so the main house was also without electricity; otherwise there could well have been a chain reaction which would have burnt down the main farmhouse too, with the Aged FIL therein.

Although I had unplugged the compressor from the mains after inflating the tractor tyres – and indeed as I usually do after using any of his equipment – the strain on the ancient, cloth-wrapped wiring had obviously finally proved to be too much.

The silly thing is, although the Aged FIL wears an emergency aid button on his wrist, he didn't think of pressing it.

"I heard loud bangs, and saw lots of smoke," he said sheepishly. "At first I thought it was a fire in the chimney. But I didn't want to bother M&O." (As a reminder, the way the emergency button works is that the central control station telephones us first, then M&O, then one of the carers, and if no response is forthcoming from any of these, the fire brigade. And as luck would have it, the last two times he has pushed the button, we were unavailable, so on both occasions M&O responded.)

LSS drily pointed out that M&O had volunteered to be on the list, and would not have done so if they had not been prepared to help.

The loud bangs he had heard were exploding paint tins, as these were stored on a shelf above the electrical cabinet. Well, I call it an electrical cabinet. It was a piece of wood with wires draped around it; some of them with plug sockets dangling freely.

The *garde champêtre* had spoken to the chap from EDF, who recommended that a local electrician should be called.

When he arrived, he asked to be shown the main distribution board for the house. Seeing it, he turned quite pale. The wooden board-with-wires-and-loose-sockets in the collapsed garage was nothing when compared to the main distribution board. This is in a small external addition to the house, which used to be the Aged FIL's office. To put it bluntly, the room is a mess. There is a long home-made table against one wall, simply covered with papers and rubbish. Dead torch batteries peek out from underneath old rags; and discarded ceramic fuses are scattered around. Burnt-out light-bulbs have been carefully replaced in their cardboard packets and reside dustily between sundry jam-jars filled with rusty nails. Broken padlocks with mismatched keys fight for space amongst plastic bags containing brand-new long-sleeved shirts which have been nibbled by mice. Leaky Wellington boots badly repaired with bicycle patches, dead transistor radios, old non-working electric shavers, broken flash-lights, and an old typewriter can be seen if you look carefully. And that's just the table. I'm not even going to describe the open-fronted cupboard or open-fronted filing cabinet.

And the number of electrical bodges which the Aged FIL has done to the main electricity supply over the years simply needed to be seen to be believed. There are wires absolutely everywhere, all colour-coded appropriately to whichever colour the Aged FIL happened to lay his hands on at the time.

The head of the fire brigade also had a look at this electrical nightmare; then held an impromptu meeting with the other officialdom present viz. the electrician, EDF, and the police. The conclusion was that the wiring was unfit for use. The meeting was then re-convened in the Aged FIL's bedroom, where he was told that if he does not promise to upgrade it as soon as possible, his house will be declared uninhabitable; and he'll have to go into an old-age home. Suitably abashed, he agreed.

The local electrician then gingerly approached the main electrical installation, dug out his miner's helmet complete with LED head-torch and got busy in the gloom to ensure that at least the kitchen and bedroom had a temporary electricity supply for the Aged FIL's myriad of heaters.

On Monday LSS will be busy on the telephone, getting estimates for the electrical upgrade, speaking to the insurance company etc. etc. Unfortunately (or fortunately, depending on which way you look at it,) this is the last straw. If the Aged FIL changes his mind – which he's quite capable of doing – and refuses to have his electrical wiring upgraded once he gets the estimate, LSS will have no option but to contact the police and EDF in order to have the building officially declared uninhabitable; and the Aged FIL will then be re-homed to a retirement house in the village – whether he likes it or not – for his own safety.

So what about the rabbits, then? Well, the nest has finally fallen flat, so the little ones are now fully visible. We have ten. Seven black ones, and three caramel-coloured like their mother. Their names? Mustard, Prunes, Left Slipper, Right Slipper, Waistcoat One, Waistcoat Two... Only kidding. No, they haven't been given names; after all, they're not pets but food. Although when we next saw T&M, M's daughter promptly christened one of them *"Pot-au-feu"*. Which is a French stew. Interesting to see that French children seem to rate food as a higher priority than pets.

We then had a day of heavy rain. In the afternoon, we had lightning and thunder, with even heavier downpours. And in the evening the Aged FIL pushed his emergency button.

This time LSS was home to take the call. He was once again without electricity. It wasn't a neighbourhood power cut this time, but his mains box had tripped. LSS checked all the old ceramic fuses without success and finally in desperation gave the festoon of wiring around the old mains box a shake. This seemed to resolve the problem. I had a feeling that this was a temporary fix.

I was proved correct. The next day, the carer telephoned us in the late afternoon. Surprise! The Aged FIL has no electricity again. We drove over to investigate.

Using my multimeter to trace the fault, it appeared that during his attempts to restore power to the Aged FIL's premises after the recent fire-and-power-failure, the electrician had dislodged an electrical junction trunking leading (eventually) to a plug socket in the kitchen. The one which powers two electric heaters. Yes, I know, I know. The old cloth-wrapped wiring had shorted out. I isolated the short, replaced the fuse wire in the ceramic fuse – using the very last piece of fuse wire – and put a piece of duct tape over the plug socket to prevent it from being used. The heaters were transferred to the washing machine plug socket, which is the only other electrical outlet in the kitchen. I'm not counting the other two plug sockets bodged into the 10-Amp lighting circuit.

The following day's post included a receipt, indicating that HSBC had received the recorded letter requesting the closure of my bank account.

In the afternoon we paid a visit to BricoDepot in Orleans to obtain sundry building supplies which will enable me to start work on constructing the corridor between the lounge and the barn. Once the solar panel installation has been completed, that is. The corridor construction entails building a partition wall and door in the bedroom, before I use a hammer and chisel to open up an entrance into the barn.

Other items on the shopping list now include an air compressor; because the Aged FIL's is now a melted pile of scrap due to the fire, and a small generator to power our essentials should there be another long-lasting electricity outage – which, with the current state of the weather, is highly likely.

Shopping at BricoDepot is both a good and bad experience.

- Good; because they usually have items in stock. Except for today, of course. The generator I wanted had sold out, so I'll need to pay a visit to the branch in Bourges tomorrow to get that. But it's at a good price, so it's worth the trip.

- Bad; because although BricoDepot is owned by the Kingfisher Group which also owns B&Q and Screwfix in the UK, the customer service (ah, those foreign words again) is typically French.

Their stock is placed on heavy-duty racking, reaching to the ceiling in some places. I asked for some assistance in retrieving ten timber beams from a high stack, just out of reach. Assistance was promised.

Having waited for nearly ten minutes, LSS then joined me, having been wandering around on her own looking for other bits and pieces. Successfully, I may add. She went off to ask for assistance. Assistance was promised.

After yet another ten minutes, she went to ask again. Finally a fork-lift truck operator appeared. Unfortunately his forklift was already heavily-laden with another customer's purchases. He joined the queue waiting to pay, which by this time had grown enormously. I'd had enough. I climbed onto the lowest stack of timbers, and at the full extent of my arms, pulled the beams I required from the upper stack one at a time. It's a good job I'm tall. The fork-lift truck operator watched this operation expressionlessly, then said something like "Do you need assistance?"

"*Désolé, je ne parle pas français!*" (Sorry, I don't speak French), I retorted, then added in English, "When we asked for help, you lot couldn't be bothered. Now you can bu**er off; I'll do it myself." Uncomprehending Gallic shrugs resulted.

(When we had finally paid for all our purchases and left the shop with two fully-laden heavy-duty trolleys, we noticed a group of five employees in the car-park all chatting away and smoking cigarettes. Now as an ex-smoker myself, I have no issue with people taking smoke-breaks. But when a shop is busy and there are insufficient staff, as a manager I would not countenance having five employees taking a break at the same time).

Having loaded the timber beams onto the trolley, we moved on to the aisle containing doors. At this point LSS received a telephone call from *Présence Verte* on her mobile. The Aged FIL had pushed his emergency button.

Again.

Obviously, as we were in Orleans, LSS requested that the next person on the list – M&O – respond to the call. It later transpired that there had been a thunderstorm, and the Aged FIL's electricity supply had tripped.

Again.

M&O managed to reset it successfully. Eventually. You see, M had never been in the Aged FIL's office before, and it took him quite a while to figure out which ceramic fuse was which underneath all the wiring. We've received an estimate from the company for which LSS's cousin's husband works (well, it's the countryside; everybody either knows everybody else or is related) for the re-wiring of the Aged FIL's house. It's around €4500, which is roughly what I estimated it would cost. The Aged FIL will be able to afford that, so as soon as the second estimate is received from the emergency electrician who attended last Saturday we'll be able to authorise the work. This emergency-button-pushing due to failing electrics has to stop!

Later, when LSS visited the other farmhouse to check that the electricity was still functioning, the Aged FIL was Not a Happy Bunny. According to him, M&O had spent far too much time in the office fixing the fuse. He had therefore obviously been snooping through all the Aged FIL's papers; despite the fact that these related to a business which had closed down some 20 years previously. LSS did not take kindly to this criticism of M&O, pointing out that firstly, it would have been difficult to actually find any business papers in the complete mess; secondly, if the Aged FIL had listened to reason previously and had the electricity supply upgraded he would not be having all these problems; and thirdly, if it hadn't been for M&O two years ago, the Aged FIL would not be here today. They had found him collapsed on the kitchen floor one winter's morning. He had spent the night there having been unable to get up because he had decided to stop eating.

I then received a bit of good news; a refund from the French National Health Service for my dental filling, which brought the cost down to a meagre €17. When later we mentioned this to T&M, they did point out that in contrast to dental work, there is a six-month wait if you would like to have a check-up at an optometrist – and unless you have a *"Mutuelle"* which is a top-up healthcare payment, spectacles are horribly expensive. The annual cost of the *"Mutuelle"* itself is also rather high, so we've opted to do without. As we're planning a visit to the UK towards the end of the year to stock up on some essentials, we'll try and book an appointment at Vision Express for an eye test. Not that either of us need spectacles yet, but it would be nice to have an official verdict!

I went to the other branch of BricoDepot in Bourges, on my own this time, as LSS had Things To Do. She had called them first to make sure they had this model of generator in stock (they did) and to ask if they would reserve one for me ("Yes," they said). So we now have a means of pushing electrons through some copper wires if there's another power cut!

We paid another visit to the village polling station, this time to vote in the EU elections. The turnout did not seem to be as impressive as it was when the local Mayoral elections were being held! Once again the French system appears to be particularly unkind to trees; each party – of which there were many! - has its own piece of paper. Not only do you receive a parcel of these in the post beforehand, but on voting day these same pieces of paper are displayed in stacks on two trestle tables. One collects a piece of paper from each stack, and in the secrecy of the polling booth puts one's chosen piece of paper in the envelope. The unused pieces of paper are then simply thrown away. Of course in our case they were thrown away in the direction of the box containing fire-lighting materials.

The little bunnies are now eating solid food in addition to their accustomed diet; so we now need to pick grass, dandelions, clover etc. etc. several times a day. They're also tucking in to kitchen vegetable scraps, like radish leaves, for example. Speaking of bunnies, here's a rather chilling bunny-related tale. (The following had to be scrutinised by LSS, because she wanted to check some details first.) Details have now been checked and verified, so here it is:

Once upon a time, LSS had a First Cousin Twice Removed. To save you looking it up in a genealogical textbook, this was her grandfather's cousin. During the Second World War, most of France was of course occupied by the Germans.

In fact some were billeted fairly close to the Aged FIL's farm. Of course this meant the soldiers were constant visitors, grabbing any food available in order to supplement their rations, until there was only a solitary male pig left in the pigsty. The Aged FIL's father managed to keep possession of this boar by saying the only two words of German he knew. "*Nicht Gut! Nicht Gut!*" ("No good!" (for eating)). The Aged FIL was a lad of around seven at this time, and was constantly following the soldiers around, asking for chocolate, much to the horror of his elder sister, the Aged Aunt.

Anyway, one of the laws that the occupying forces had imposed was that the possession of firearms was prohibited, for obvious reasons.

Now this First Cousin Twice Removed (we'll call him Charles, because not only was that his name, but to keep referring to him as First Cousin Twice Removed would be silly) was a farmer. He would have been in his late thirties when the following events occurred. He was also particularly fond of wild rabbits. I don't mean he went into the woods to admire the cute bunnies; I mean that he found them to be extremely tasty, especially when his wife Albertine made a casserole on the wood-burning kitchen range. As his skills at setting snares were not really up to scratch, he decided to ignore this apparently stupid law, and retained his shotgun. All would have been well, had Charles not also had a fondness for a few glasses of lunchtime wine at the pavement tables of the village café. On this particular day he had arranged to meet his friend René, to catch up on some gossip.

=======

The sunlight sparkled on the wine-glasses of the two men. An open packet of Gauloises cigarettes lay next to a half-empty bottle of red wine, which cast a ruby shadow on the surface of the stained circular table. The state of the ashtray indicated that the men had been there for some time; two empty wine-bottles had already been removed by the waiter. Deep in conversation, the two men paid scant attention to the other customers. The sunlight also glittered on the silver-grey braid around the collar of *Scharführer* Günzel[13], seated at a table near the doorway. Although the local radar installation fell under the jurisdiction of the Luftwaffe, *Scharführer* Günzel had been seconded to this unit. He was ostensibly in charge of the security for the radar; but the real reason for his posting was to try and gather any intelligence available regarding the local French Resistance.

The nearby *Maquis de Souesmes* were giving the occupying forces a lot of trouble. The munitions factory in nearby Salbris was now under German control, and the four main sections of this factory were linked by a rail network; an easy target for sabotage.

The diamond-shaped patch on his uniform sleeve bore the letters "SD" (*Sicherheitsdienst*); *Scharführer* Günzel was a non-commissioned officer in the SS. He had been selected for this particular task because he spoke fluent French, although as part of his cover he pretended not to understand more than a few basic words.

The conversation between Charles and his friend was becoming interesting. René was complaining about the scarcity of the local game, and the recent difficulty in snaring rabbits. "I don't have that problem!" boasted Charles. "I just use my shotgun. I'm not obeying any stupid *Boche* rules. My farm is miles away from the village, so nobody is any the wiser." His friend kicked him under the table, indicating the German soldier drinking coffee at the table near the doorway. "Oh,

---

[13]This name is fictitious. It was the name of my high-school German language teacher, whom I disliked. Obviously there is no easy way to trace which German SS NCO it was. The rest of the tale is true.

don't worry about him," he hiccupped. "He's always here. He doesn't speak French anyway. More wine?"

A few days later, Charles was not at home when a squad of German soldiers arrived to search for the illegal shotgun. But his wife was.

The children were somewhat puzzled to find their mother missing when they returned home from school. She was never seen again; she died in Dachau. There is a simple plaque on her parents' grave:

"En mémoire de Albertine
morte en Allemagne
à 35 Ans
Regrets"

(In memory of Albertine
died in Germany
aged 35 years
Regrets)

========

(Postscript: When Charles died in 1985, his children refused to have him buried in the family plot. Instead he is interred at the other end of the village cemetery, as far away from the family plot as they could get.)

We would appear to have a coypu in our pond. This is both good and bad news. Good, because we can make some more pâté and tanning-of-skin; and bad, because these animals are very habitat-destructive if not caught. We can do without ring-barked trees and increased erosion of the pond banks due to tunnelling, thank you very much. I'll need to set up the Aged FIL's live trap tomorrow. This is a wire cage with a base-plate linked to sliding doors at both ends. When an animal steps on the base-plate, the doors shut. Unfortunately disposing of the animal humanely is going to be a problem. It's considered a pest, and is an exotic species.

A long, long, time ago I owned a .22LR pistol, which I enjoyed using for occasional target shooting. Unfortunately the UK government decided this was A Bad Thing, and banned pistol ownership. Of course this meant the end of gun crime in the UK.

Oh, wait, wrong universe. Of course it didn't.

Anyway, having surrendered the pistol to the authorities as required by law, I purchased a .22LR rifle instead. Unfortunately the UK government then promptly decided this was also A Bad Thing, and changed the rules. One had to be a member of a shooting club, and attend regular meetings. Regular, as in weekly. Due to time constraints at the time, I was unable to comply with the weekly requirement, so that was the end of my target shooting days.

.22 ownership is Frowned Upon in France; I could apply for a hunting licence, and get a shotgun or larger calibre rifle but I don't have the time or finances at the moment. The point is: I am left without a humane way of dispatching the possibly-caught coypu. As it is an environmental destroyer, releasing it elsewhere is not an option – and would actually be illegal. And even if I had a shotgun, this would damage both the meat and the pelt. Whacking it on the head with an iron bar could be dangerous; these animals can inflict a nasty bite when cornered. But I may not have any other option. I'll say no more, but I'm afraid there will be no quick method employed, if the animal is unfortunate enough to get caught in the trap.

LSS later had the bright idea of searching the Aged FIL's cupboards for a suitable coypu dispatcher. Success! We have now borrowed something which I must admit I have never seen before. It's called a "garden gun".

It's a single-shot shotgun. In other words the barrel has no rifling. But it's bolt-action, and takes a selection of 9mm rimfire cartridges. Those of particular interest in this case are solid slugs. Now at least we have a humane method of disposing of the coypu. Should we catch it, of course. The live trap has been placed at the back of the pond.

There has still been no news from HSBC regarding the bank account closure. The remaining funds have still not been transferred to our joint account. LSS called them to enquire what the delay was. They replied that everything was in order, but it could take up to a month to close an account. Why am I not surprised?

Towards the end of the month, the one remaining wall of the Aged FIL's garage fell down. Well, at least that saves us having to get someone to demolish it. The insurance expert had paid us a visit, and said we can start getting quotes for rebuilding.

Wildlife diary: The male and female ducks are still visiting the pond every day, but despite walking around the entire pond we have not been able to find a new nest, so perhaps they've decided against trying to raise another batch of ducklings here this year.

And the coypu has not been seen for a few days now. The trap had been baited with some potatoes, but LSS bought an apple today at the supermarket, so we've replaced the potatoes with pieces of apple. Hopefully it's moved on to other premises. If not, we'll eat it.

About the Author

Robert Martin was born in Uganda in 1963. He graduated with a BSc degree in Forestry and Nature Conservation in 1987. He has also been in Kenya, Tanzania, Australia, South Africa, Namibia and the United Kingdom.

He now resides in France with his wife Caroline, where he is currently renovating a nineteenth century farmhouse, and attempting to learn the French words for sundry building materials.

Author of the money-saving guide "How To Survive a Recession", he is also the creator and administrator of several websites:

http://www.st-1100.com
http://www.landyrebuild.com
http://www.stampswops.com
http://www.la-darnoire.com